THE MARIJUANA DUI HANDBOOK

DAVID N. JOLLY

The opinions expressed in this manuscript are solely the opinions of the author and do not represent the opinions or thoughts of the publisher. The author has represented and warranted full ownership and/or legal right to publish all the materials in this book.

The Marijuana DUI Handbook
All Rights Reserved.
Copyright © 2014 David N. Jolly
v3.0

Cover Photo © 2014 thinkstockphotos.com. All rights reserved - used with permission.

This book may not be reproduced, transmitted, or stored in whole or in part by any means, including graphic, electronic, or mechanical without the express written consent of the publisher except in the case of brief quotations embodied in critical articles and reviews.

Outskirts Press, Inc.
http://www.outskirtspress.com

ISBN: 978-1-4787-0578-9

Outskirts Press and the "OP" logo are trademarks belonging to Outskirts Press, Inc.

PRINTED IN THE UNITED STATES OF AMERICA

For my wife and son

David N. Jolly is also the author of:

The DUI Handbook for the Accused (2007)
DUI/DWI: The History of Driving Under the Influence (2009)
The DUI Handbook for the Accused II (2010)
The Drug DUI Handbook (2011)
The DUI Investigation Handbook (2011)
The Ultimate Washington State DUI Handbook (2011)
The Traffic Ticket Handbook (2011)
The Washington State DUI Pocket Handbook (2012)
The Whatcom County DUI Handbook (2013)
The Snohomish County DUI Handbook (2013)
The Skagit County DUI Handbook (2013)
The Island County DUI Handbook (2013)
The King County DUI Handbook (2013)

Table of Contents

Preface ix

Introduction 1

CHAPTER 1
Marijuana and Its Effect on the Body 6

CHAPTER 2
Marijuana and Its Effect on Driving 14

CHAPTER 3
Field Sobriety Tests to Detect Marijuana 27

CHAPTER 4
Drug Recognition Experts (DRE) 55

CHAPTER 5
Blood Testing for Marijuana 77

CHAPTER 6
Marijuana Dependency and Treatment 86

Bibliography 91

Preface

A Brief Introduction to Marijuana
Cannabis / Marijuana
(Δ^9-Tetrahydrocannabinol, THC)

Marijuana is a green or gray mixture of dried shredded flowers and leaves of the hemp plant *Cannabis sativa*. Hashish consists of resinous secretions of the cannabis plant. Dronabinol (synthetic THC) is a light yellow resinous oil.

Synonyms: Cannabis, marijuana, pot, reefer, buds, grass, weed, dope, ganja, herb, boom, gangster, Mary Jane, sinsemilla, shit, joint, hash, hash oil, blow, blunt, green, kilobricks, Thai sticks; Marinol®

Source: Cannabis contains chemicals called cannabinoids, including cannabinol, cannabidiol, cannabinolidic acids, cannabigerol, cannabichromene, and several isomers of tetrahydrocannabinol (THC). One of these isomers, Δ^9-THC, is believed to be responsible for most of the characteristic psychoactive effects of cannabis. Marijuana refers to the leaves and flowering tops of the cannabis plant; the buds are often preferred because of their higher THC content. Hashish consists of the THC-rich resinous secretions of the plant, which are collected, dried, compressed and smoked. Hashish oil is produced by extracting the cannabinoids from plant material with a solvent. In the U. S., marijuana, hashish and hashish oil are Schedule I controlled substances. Dronabinol (Marinol®) is a Schedule III controlled substance and is available in strengths of 2.5, 5 or 10 mg in round, soft gelatin capsules.

Drug Class: *Cannabis/ Marijuana*: spectrum of behavioral effects is unique, preventing classification of the drug as a stimulant, sedative, tranquilizer, or hallucinogen. *Dronabinol*: appetite stimulant, antiemetic.

Medical and Recreational Uses: *Medicinal*: Indicated for the treatment of anorexia associated with weight loss in patients with AIDS, and to treat mild to moderate nausea and vomiting associated with cancer chemotherapy. *Recreational*: Marijuana is used for its mood altering effects, euphoria, and relaxation. Marijuana is the most commonly used illicit drug throughout the world.

Potency, Purity and Dose: THC is the major psychoactive constituent of cannabis. Potency is dependent on THC concentration and is usually expressed as %THC per dry weight of material. Average THC concentration in marijuana is 1-5%, hashish 5-15%, and hashish oil ³ 20%. The form of marijuana known as *sinsemilla* is derived from the unpollinated female cannabis plant and is preferred for its high THC content (up to 17% THC). Recreational doses are highly variable and users often titer their own dose. A single intake of smoke from a pipe or joint is called a hit (approximately 1/20th of a gram). The lower the potency or THC content the more hits are needed to achieve the desired effects; 1-3 hits of high potency sinsemilla is typically enough to produce the desired effects. In terms of its psychoactive effect, a drop or two of hash oil on a cigarette is equal to a single "joint" of marijuana. Medicinally, the initial starting dose of Marinol® is 2.5 mg, twice daily.

Route of Administration: Marijuana is usually smoked as a cigarette ('joint') or in a pipe or bong. Hollowed out cigars packed with marijuana are also common and are called `. Joints and blunts are often laced with adulterants including PCP or crack cocaine. Joints can also be dipped in liquid PCP or in codeine cough syrup. Marijuana is also orally ingested.

Pharmacodynamics: THC binds to cannabinoid receptors and interferes with important endogenous cannabinoid neurotransmitter systems. Receptor distribution correlates with brain areas involved in physiological, psychomotor and cognitive effects. Correspondingly, THC produces alterations in motor behavior, perception, cognition, memory, learning, endocrine function, food intake, and regulation of body temperature.

Pharmacokinetics: Absorption is slower following the oral route of administration with lower, more delayed peak THC levels. Bioavailability is reduced following oral ingestion due to extensive first pass metabolism. Smoking marijuana results in rapid absorption with peak THC plasma concentrations occurring prior to the end of smoking. Concentrations vary depending on the potency of marijuana and the manner in which the drug is smoked, however, peak plasma concentrations of 100-200 ng/mL are routinely encountered. Plasma THC concentrations generally fall below 5 ng/mL less than 3 hours after smoking. THC is highly lipid soluble, and plasma and urinary elimination half-lives are best estimated at 3-4 days, where the rate-limiting step is the slow redistribution to plasma of THC sequestered in the tissues. Shorter half-lives are generally reported due to limited collection intervals and less sensitive analytical methods. Plasma THC concentrations in occasional users rapidly fall below limits of quantitation within 8 to 12 h. THC is rapidly and extensively metabolized with very little THC being excreted unchanged from the body. THC is primarily metabolized to 11-hydroxy-THC which has equipotent psychoactivity. The 11-hydroxy-THC is then rapidly metabolized to the 11-nor-9-carboxy-THC (THC-COOH) which is not psychoactive. A majority of THC is excreted via the feces (~65%) with approximately 30% of the THC being eliminated in the urine as conjugated glucuronic acids and free THC hydroxylated metabolites.

Molecular Interactions / Receptor Chemistry: THC is metabolized via cytochrome P450 2C9, 2C11, and 3A isoenzymes. Potential inhibitors of these isoenzymes could decrease the rate of THC elimination if administered concurrently, while potential inducers could increase the rate of elimination.

Blood to Plasma Concentration Ratio: 0.55

Interpretation of Blood Concentrations: It is difficult to establish a relationship between a person's

THC blood or plasma concentration and performance impairing effects. Concentrations of parent drug and metabolite are very dependent on pattern of use as well as dose. THC concentrations typically peak during the act of smoking, while peak 11-OH THC concentrations occur approximately 9-23 minutes after the start of smoking. Concentrations of both analytes decline rapidly and are often < 5 ng/mL at 3 hours. Significant THC concentrations (7 to 18 ng/mL) are noted following even a single puff or hit of a marijuana cigarette. Peak plasma THC concentrations ranged from 46-188 ng/mL in 6 subjects after they smoked 8.8 mg THC over 10 minutes. Chronic users can have mean plasma levels of THC-COOH of 45 ng/mL, 12 hours after use; corresponding THC levels are, however, less than 1 ng/mL. Following oral administration, THC concentrations peak at 1-3 hours and are lower than after smoking. Dronabinol and THC-COOH are present in equal concentrations in plasma and concentrations peak at approximately 2-4 hours after dosing.

It is inadvisable to try and predict effects based on blood THC concentrations alone, and currently impossible to predict specific effects based on THC-COOH concentrations. It is possible for a person to be affected by marijuana use with concentrations of THC in their blood below the limit of detection of the method. Mathematical models have been developed to estimate the time of marijuana exposure within a 95% confidence interval. Knowing the elapsed time from marijuana exposure can then be used to predict impairment in concurrent cognitive and psychomotor effects based on data in the published literature.

Interpretation of Urine Test Results: Detection of total THC metabolites in urine, primarily THC-COOH-glucuronide, only indicates prior THC exposure. Detection time is well past the window of intoxication and impairment. Published excretion data from controlled clinical studies may provide a reference for evaluating urine cannabinoid concentrations; however, these data are generally reflective of occasional marijuana use rather than heavy, chronic marijuana exposure. It can take as long as 4 hours for THC-COOH to appear in the urine at concentrations sufficient to trigger an immunoassay (at 50ng/mL) following smoking. Positive test results generally indicate use within 1-3 days; however, the detection window could be significantly longer following heavy, chronic, use. Following single doses of Marinol®, low levels of dronabinol metabolites have been detected for more than 5 weeks in urine. Low concentrations of THC have also been measured in over-the-counter hemp oil products – consumption of these products may produce positive urine cannabinoid test results.

Effects: Pharmacological effects of marijuana vary with dose, route of administration, experience of user, vulnerability to psychoactive effects, and setting of use.

Psychological: At recreational doses, effects include relaxation, euphoria, relaxed inhibitions, sense of well-being, disorientation, altered time and space perception, lack of concentration, impaired learning and memory, alterations in thought formation and expression, drowsiness, sedation, mood changes such as panic reactions and paranoia, and a more vivid sense of taste, sight, smell, and hearing. Stronger doses intensify reactions and may cause fluctuating emotions, flights of fragmentary thoughts with disturbed associations, a dulling of attention despite an illusion of heightened insight, image distortion, and psychosis.

Physiological: The most frequent effects include increased heart rate, reddening of the eyes, dry mouth and throat, increased appetite, and vasodilatation.

Side Effect Profile: Fatigue, paranoia, possible psychosis, memory problems, depersonalization, mood alterations, urinary retention, constipation, decreased motor coordination, lethargy, slurred speech, and dizziness. Impaired health including lung damage, behavioral changes, and reproductive, cardiovascular and immunological effects have been associated with regular marijuana use. Regular and chronic marijuana smokers may have many of the same respiratory problems that tobacco smokers have (daily cough and phlegm, symptoms of chronic bronchitis), as the amount of tar inhaled and the level of carbon monoxide absorbed by marijuana smokers is 3 to 5 times greater than among tobacco smokers. Smoking marijuana while shooting up cocaine has the potential to cause severe increases in heart rate and blood pressure.

Duration of Effects: Effects from smoking cannabis products are felt within minutes and reach their peak in 10-30 minutes. Typical marijuana smokers experience a high that lasts approximately 2 hours. Most behavioral and physiological effects return to baseline levels within 3-5 hours after drug use, although some investigators have demonstrated residual effects in specific behaviors up to 24 hours, such as complex divided attention tasks. Psychomotor impairment can persist after the perceived high has dissipated. In long term users, even after periods of abstinence, selective attention (ability to filter out irrelevant information) has been shown to be adversely affected with increasing duration of use, and speed of information processing has been shown to be impaired with increasing frequency of use. Dronabinol has an onset of

30-60 minutes, peak effects occur at 2-4 hours, and it can stimulate the appetite for up to 24 hours.

Tolerance, Dependence and Withdrawal Effect: Tolerance may develop to some pharmacological effects of dronabinol. Tolerance to many of the effects of marijuana may develop rapidly after only a few doses, but also disappears rapidly. Marijuana is addicting as it causes compulsive drug craving, seeking, and use, even in the face of negative health and social consequences. Additionally, animal studies suggests marijuana causes physical dependence. A withdrawal syndrome is commonly seen in chronic marijuana users following abrupt discontinuation. Symptoms include restlessness, irritability, mild agitation, hyperactivity, insomnia, nausea, cramping, decreased appetite, sweating, and increased dreaming.

Drug Interactions: Cocaine and amphetamines may lead to increased hypertension, tachycardia and possible cardiotoxicity. Benzodiazepines, barbiturates, ethanol, opioids, antihistamines, muscle relaxants and other CNS depressants increase drowsiness and CNS depression. When taken concurrently with alcohol, marijuana is more likely to be a traffic safety risk factor than when consumed alone.

Performance Effects: The short term effects of marijuana use include problems with memory and learning, distorted perception, difficultly in thinking and problem-solving, and loss of coordination. Heavy users may have increased difficulty sustaining attention, shifting attention to meet the demands of changes in the environment, and in registering, processing and using information. In general, laboratory performance studies indicate that sensory functions are not highly impaired, but perceptual functions are significantly affected. The ability to concentrate and maintain attention are decreased during marijuana use, and impairment of hand-eye coordination is dose-related over a wide range of dosages. Impairment in retention time and tracking, subjective sleepiness, distortion of time and distance, vigilance, and loss of coordination in divided attention tasks have been reported. Note however, that subjects can often "pull themselves together" to concentrate on simple tasks for brief periods of time. Significant performance impairments are usually observed for at least 1-2 hours following marijuana use, and residual effects have been reported up to 24 hours.

Effects on Driving: The drug manufacturer suggests that patients receiving treatment with Marinol® should be specifically warned not to drive until it is established that they are able to tolerate the drug and perform such tasks safely. Epidemiology data from road traffic arrests and fatalities indicate that after alcohol, marijuana is the most frequently detected psychoactive substance among driving populations. Marijuana has been shown to impair performance on driving simulator tasks and on open and closed driving courses for up to approximately 3 hours. Decreased car handling performance, increased reaction times, impaired time and distance estimation, inability to maintain headway, lateral travel, subjective sleepiness, motor incoordination, and impaired sustained vigilance have all been reported. Some drivers may actually be able to improve performance for brief periods by overcompensating for self-perceived impairment. The greater the demands placed on the driver, however, the more critical the likely impairment. Marijuana may particularly impair monotonous and prolonged driving. Decision times to evaluate situations and determine appropriate responses increase. Mixing alcohol and marijuana may dramatically produce effects greater than either drug on its own.

DEC Category: Cannabis

DEC Profile: Horizontal gaze nystagmus not present; vertical gaze nystagmus not present; lack of convergence present; pupil size normal to dilated; reaction to light normal to slow; pulse rate elevated; blood pressure elevated; body temperature normal to elevated. Other characteristic indicators may include odor of marijuana in car or on subject's breath, marijuana debris in mouth, green coating of tongue, bloodshot eyes, body and eyelid tremors, relaxed inhibitions, incomplete thought process, and poor performance on field sobriety tests.

Panel's Assessment of Driving Risks: Low doses of THC moderately impair cognitive and psychomotor tasks associated with driving, while severe driving impairment is observed with high doses, chronic use and in combination with low doses of alcohol The more difficult and unpredictable the task, the more likely marijuana will impair performance.

Source of information: http://www.nhtsa.gov/People/injury/research/job185drugs/cannabis.htm

Introduction

Marijuana is now legal to consume recreationally in both the State of Washington and the State of Colorado. It is assumed that in the very near future many more states will follow and legalize the recreational use of marijuana. The states rumored to be next in legalizing the recreational use of marijuana include Oregon, California, Nevada, Rhode Island, Maine, Alaska and Vermont. The subject of marijuana as a legalized recreational drug is increasing in potency and the days of demonizing the drug are numbered in most states.

The use of marijuana for medicinal purposes is already legal in Alaska, Hawaii, Oregon, California, Nevada, Arizona, Montana, Michigan, Vermont, Maine, Massachusetts, Rhode Island, Connecticut, New Jersey, Delaware and Washington D.C., in addition to the already mentioned States of Washington and Colorado. It is expected than many more states will be added to this list in the very near future as advocates of medicinal marijuana are finding voice in local, state and federal politics.

However, the liberalization of marijuana consumption has caused concern in law enforcement, prosecuting attorney offices and many politicians. As a result, and to address the fears of many, new marijuana DUI laws are being created to fend off the perceived epidemic that law enforcement believes is coming.

In 2012, Washington State amended its driving under the influence statute to include language that makes it illegal to operate or be in physical control of a vehicle if the "[t]he person has, within two hours after driving, a THC concentration of 5.00 or higher as shown by analysis of the person's blood..." Following Washington's lead, Colorado passed a Marijuana DUI Bill in 2013 which mirrors the Washington State marijuana DUI law. Times they are a-changin'.

It is presumed that any State that legalizes the recreational use of marijuana will amend their respective DUI/DWI statutes to reflect similar language and to ease the fears of law enforcement and politicians.

In the driving under the influence (DUI) context it is conceded that marijuana may impair perception, memory, judgment, motor skills, and the ability to

INTRODUCTION | 3

operate a motor vehicle. According to governmental statistics from the National Highway Traffic Safety Administration (NHTSA), about one in five (18 percent) motorists killed in 2010 had drugs in their system at the time of the crash. http://www.whitehousedrugpolicy.gov

While this data did not distinguish whether drugs were a factor in the accidents, nor did it indicate how many of the motorists were in fact under the influence of drugs at the time of the crash, it nonetheless does raise questions about drug use by motorists.

Recent surveys have suggested how pervasive drugged driving has become in the United States. *The National Roadside Survey of Alcohol and Drug Use by Drivers*, a nationally representative survey by NHTSA, found that in 2007, 16 percent of weekend nighttime drivers (roughly one in six) tested positive for legal or illegal drugs.

White House Drug Policy Director Gil Kerlikowske acknowledged the limits of the data, while insisting there is a "significant problem" of drugged driving in the US:

> We've made great progress on alcohol-impaired driving through education and enforcement. There's just no reason we won't be able to make progress in this area once we start bringing it to people's attention and we start doing the enforcement that's needed.

Due to the many changes in law in both Washington and Colorado, and the perceived changes in many more States in the upcoming years regarding the legalization of marijuana and the corresponding amendments to DUI laws, driving under the influence of marijuana will become an increasingly well studied area. This will undoubtedly result in greater emphasis on drug DUI enforcement within police departments and greater understanding by prosecuting attorneys on how to successfully prosecute such crimes.

Investigating a driver for possible marijuana impairment begins prior to contacting the driver with observations of driving and continues throughout contact to the point of chemical testing of the driver's blood. In most respects detecting the marijuana driver is very much like detecting the alcohol impaired driver. In this regard the officer makes observations of the demeanor and physical appearance of the driver, coordination and motor skills based on field sobriety tests, and later chemical evidence by way of a blood draw. Further, there is a commonality between the two as both alcohol and marijuana can impair a person's ability to drive. However, the detection of the alcohol or marijuana impaired driver deviates the moment the driver is arrested. At that point the law enforcement officer who suspects the driver is under the influence of drugs can utilize the 12-step DRE (Drug Recognition Expert) evaluation process to gather

INTRODUCTION | 5

additional evidence of possible drug impairment.

This book details the marijuana DUI process from driving behavior, field sobriety testing, the DRE 12-step process, blood draws, and an analysis of how marijuana may impair and affect an individual and their ability to drive. This book is an objective and detailed review of the process that marijuana DUI cases must go through and a comprehensive analysis of the detection of marijuana impaired drivers and the gathering of evidence to prove a driver is under the influence of marijuana. This book is a must for every DUI law enforcement officer and any individual in the DUI field, including prosecutors and DUI defense attorneys. For those who have been arrested for a marijuana DUI, this is a necessary read.

CHAPTER 1

Marijuana and Its Effect on the Body

The consumption of marijuana and its popularity is entirely the result of its narcotic or psychoactive qualities. Marijuana is an intoxicating drug, affecting conscious and unconscious mental processing and all the senses, which are controlled by the central nervous system (brain and spinal cord).

Marijuana's appeal as a recreational drug is related to one or more of the following feelings experienced by many, but not all, users after consumption: euphoria, reduced anxiety, sense of enhanced well-being, increased sensory perception, increased sociability, heightened sexual experience, and heightened creativity. Other effects experienced are similar to those associated with alcohol, and may include: unsteady gait, muscle relaxation and/or loss of muscle coordination, weakness, slurred speech, slowed reactions, impaired short-term memory, distortion of time, altered depth perception, fatigue, sedation, dysphoria, anxiety, hallucinations, depersonalization (feelings of unreality or strangeness about one's behavior), and disturbed sleep. One unique affect users may experience following the consumption of marijuana is appetite stimulation, commonly referred to as the "munchies" by marijuana users.

Importantly, as with all drugs, dosage is the key. Low doses of marijuana tend to induce relaxation, disinhibition, and decreased anxiety, whereas high doses may result in dysphoria, anxiety, panic attacks, especially in inexperienced users. Low doses also tend to increase sensory acuity, usually in a pleasurable way, whereas high doses tend to distort sensory perception and may cause hallucinations and even psychotic episodes. These are typically of short duration, especially if marijuana use is discontinued.

The effects of marijuana, like all drugs, can be traced to the chemical composition and molecular structure of the active ingredients. Tetrahydroncannabinol, or THC, one of the 60-plus cannabinoids compounds found in the *Cannabis sativa* plant, is marijuana's main active ingredient. Numerous factors determine how a drug acts in the body, including its route of administration. For example, marijuana's effects can be diminished or heightened depending on whether THC is inhaled, ingested as a pill, or administrated as a mouth spray, transdermal patch, or rectal enema. Other factors include dosage and interaction with foods or other drugs ingested or administered within the same time frame.

Technically, THC applies its effects through binding to cannabinoid receptors and interferes with the neurotransmitter release. The distribution of cannabinoid receptors in the brain and other tissues is responsible for the variety of physiological, psychomotor, and cognitive effects observed in subjects after consumption. THC in the body may produce alterations in motor function, perception, cognition, memory, learning, endocrine function, and immunity, and has other influences, some of which appear to be interrelated with other neural pathways.

The preferred route of marijuana administration by many users is smoking and this method of administration efficiently delivers THC from the lungs to the brain, resulting in a rapid onset of effects. For many marijuana smokers, the intense sense of pleasure felt almost immediately after THC exposure to the central nervous system reinforces its use. However, the dose taken when smoked can vary from person to person due to the number of puffs taken, the duration and spacing of puffs, the hold time, and volume inhaled with each puff. These variables allow the dose to be adjusted to the desired degree of effect.

THC taken orally, unlike smoked marijuana, is absorbed from the gastrointestinal tract into the intestinal circulation. In such instances nearly all of the dose (about 90% to 95%) is absorbed because of its high lipid solubility. The intestinal circulation flows directly to the liver, where THC is rapidly metabolized into other chemical compounds, and only a small amount of the dose (10% to 20%) reaches the systemic circulation. When smoked, THC readily crosses the alveolar membrane of the lungs into the blood of the pulmonary capillaries. From there it is delivered to the heart where it is pumped directly to the brain, bypassing the liver and first-pass metabolism.

When marijuana is smoked the blood concentration of THC is detectable in the blood within seconds and increases with each smoke. Once the subject has stopped smoking, the blood concentration of THC rapidly decreases because of its rapid distribution into tissues and the metabolism in the liver.

The Downside to the High Side

Marijuana's euphoric effect is the attraction of its consumption. However, like most every drug there are adverse effects to ingestion. Most of the negative aspects to using involve the effect to the body's central nervous system, circulatory system, and respiratory system, particularly for regular heavy users. THC increases heart rate and modulates blood pressure (lowers blood pressure when standing and increases blood pressure when laying down), and therefore some individuals are at increased risk of a potentially serious cardiovascular event. THC can increase the resistance to blood flow in the cerebral vasculature and therefore there is also a risk of stroke.

Other serious side effects from marijuana use include seizures, schizophrenia, and even psychosis. These corollary effects are still in the early stages of research at the structural, molecular, and behavioral levels. However, new research tools and techniques have provided evidence and some level of comprehension into marijuana's effects on brain structure, memory, and cognitive abilities. Certain studies have concluded that heavy daily marijuana use does damage brain tissue and impair mental health (particularly in individuals with mood disorders, psychosis, or a personal or family history of mental illness) (1)(2)(3) Cognitive deficits may include impaired learning, poor retention and retrieval, and perceptual abnormalities.

Marijuana use was once believed by many to be non-addictive but regular consumption of marijuana can lead to dependence and addiction, depending on the frequency and duration of use and the genetics and personality of the user. More is covered on marijuana addiction and treatment in Chapter Six of this book.

In addition to the concerns of addiction, there has also been debate whether marijuana consumption leads to the use, misuse, and abuse of other drugs. The idea that the use of an addictive substance leads to the use of other more addictive and harmful drugs is not new. However, the growing advocacy for legalizing or decriminalizing marijuana has put the theory of marijuana as a "gateway drug" in the spotlight again. Not surprisingly, there are conflicting views on this theory and even conflicting studies, which only adds to the confusion.

Marijuana as Medicine

The use of marijuana for medicinal purposes is now legal in Alaska, Hawaii, Washington, Oregon, California, Nevada, Arizona, Colorado, Montana, Michigan, Vermont, Maine, Massachusetts, Rhode Island, Connecticut, New Jersey, Delaware, and Washington D.C. The trend seems to suggest that many more states will be added to this list in the next few years despite The United States Supreme Court ruling in *United States v. Oakland Cannabis Buyers' Coop* and *Gonzales v. Raich* that the federal government has a right to regulate and criminalize cannabis, even for medical purposes. (4)(5)

Despite the trend in the United States, medical marijuana remains illegal in most states and most countries. However, many countries are beginning to entertain varying levels of decriminalization for medical usage, including Canada, Austria, Germany, Switzerland, the Netherlands, Czech Republic, Spain, Israel, Italy, Finland, and Portugal.

The physical administration of marijuana for medicinal purposes takes many forms including vaporizing or smoking dried buds, drinking or eating extracts, and taking capsules. Synthetic cannabinoids are available as prescription drugs in some countries also, including Marinol (The United States and Canada) and Cesamet (Canada, Mexico, the United Kingdom, and the United States).

Numerous studies have concluded that THC and other cannabinoids in marijuana have beneficial effects in certain disease states, including acute and chronic pain, malnutrition and wasting, glaucoma, autoimmunity, and neurodegenerative diseases like multiple sclerosis and Alzheimer's disease. Researchers have long recognized that cannabinoids have benefits as an analgesia (pain relief), antiemesis (for nausea and vomiting), and as an antiproliferative (cancer fighting).

The Institute of Medicine, a public and policy think tank chartered by the National Academy of Sciences, acknowledged the therapeutic benefits and recommends that the issue merits scientific evaluation (6):

> Psychological effects of cannabinoids such as anxiety reduction and sedation, which can influence medical benefits, should be evaluated in clinical trials. The psychological effects of cannabinoids are probably important determinants of their potential therapeutic value. They can influence symptoms indirectly which could create false impressions of the drug effect or be beneficial as a form of adjunctive therapy.

CHAPTER **2**

Marijuana and Its Effect on Driving

According to the National Highway Traffic Safety Administration (NHTSA), drugs other than alcohol (e.g., marijuana and cocaine) are involved in about 18 percent of all motor vehicle driver deaths. Further, among those who seek treatment for marijuana addiction or related problems, more than 50% report having driven while "stoned" at least once in the previous year.(1)(2) However, independent surveys have found alarmingly disparate results that indicate the percentage of road traffic accidents in which one driver tested positive for marijuana ranges from 6% to 32%. (3)(4).

The cause for such concern is due to the fact that

marijuana consumption is thought to affect attentiveness, vigilance, perception of time and speed, and use of acquired knowledge. (5)(6)(7)(8) In an analysis of 60 different studies it was concluded that marijuana may cause impairment in every performance area that can reasonably be connected with safe driving of a vehicle, such as tracking, motor coordination, visual functions, and particularly complex tasks that require divided attention. (9) However, it is important to note that some studies on marijuana's effects on reaction time have been contradictory. (10) More significantly, when marijuana and alcohol are used in combination there is the potential for additive or even multiplicative effects on impairment. (11) Consequently, on the basis of cognitive studies, it seems reasonable to propose that smoking marijuana may increase the risk of having a fatal traffic accident. A brief analysis of research and studies of marijuana must be tempered with the reality that the affects of the drug are dose dependent.

Driving is a complex task requiring the combination of various cognitive and psychomotor skills. Cognitive skills are those related to the processes of knowing, thinking, learning, and judging. In the driving context these effects include memory, perceptual skills, cognitive processing and task accuracy, reaction time, and sustained and divided attention.

One of the more frequently reported and validated behavioral effects of marijuana use is the impairment of short term memory. However, the direct link between the impairment of memory and driving impairment is difficult to quantify.

As mentioned, driving a motor vehicle requires varying levels of attention, cognitive capacity and psychomotor ability, depending on factors such as weather, road conditions, vehicle condition, other drivers, lighting, city versus highway driving, and so forth. Any decrease in physical ability or attention may negatively affect a driver's ability to safely operate a motor vehicle. The peak of cognitive impairment effects are reported to occur approximately 40-60 minutes following the ingestion of marijuana and on average last for two to three hours.

With the recent legalization of marijuana in both Washington and Colorado, the legalization in many states of medicinal marijuana and the undoubted continuation of marijuana legalization throughout the country, law enforcement will continue to educate themselves how to detect drivers who are impaired by the drug. To that end there are numerous studies that have been conducted to determine how marijuana affects driving skills and how the effect on driving differs from other drugs, such as alcohol. Although research examining this issue has gained momentum in recent years, the picture remains muddied by inconsistent findings and methodologies.

The legalization of marijuana in the United States

is a relatively recent phenomenon, yet research into the way marijuana affects individuals and drivers has been ongoing for many decades. When examining previous studies from many years ago it is important to remember that the doses of marijuana in previous tests were generally lower than in the marijuana consumed today. Australia was a pioneer in studying the effects of marijuana in the 1970s and beyond. In fact, and as a complete aside, a famous Australia television series, *Underbelly: A Tale of Two Cities*, chronicled the drug trade in the 1970s and the beating heart of marijuana distribution in the small rural town of Griffith, New South Wales.

In 2007, the Australian National Drug Strategy Household Survey (NDSHS) indicated that 2.9% of Australians over the age of 14 years had driven a motor vehicle while under the influence of illicit drugs in the previous 12 months. (12) These results were similar to those found in the United States Department of Health and Human Services national substance use surveys, where 4.4% and 4.3% of respondents in 2004 and 2005, respectively, reported having driven under the influence of illicit drugs in the last 12 months.

Specific to marijuana, several researchers have surveyed the driving population about their use of the drug and driving. Three independent studies out of Canada have determined between 1.5% and 2.9% of drivers having driven a vehicle during the previous 12 months under the influence of marijuana. (13)(14)(15) In Europe, the European Monitoring Centre for Drugs and Drug Addiction (EMCDDA) determined that between 0.3% and 7.4% of drivers tested positive for marijuana across seven roadside surveys conducted between 1997 and 2007 in Australia, Denmark, the Netherlands, Norway, the United Kingdom, and the United States. (16)

Researchers in Scotland concluded that among the 537 drivers surveyed, 15% of 17 to 39 year-olds and 3% of over 40 year-olds reported having ever driven within 12 hours after using marijuana. (17) In a similar study in Canada, these rates were as high as 19.7%. (14)(18) In British studies of younger people with drivers' licenses, self-reported rates of having ever driven under the influence of marijuana were 59% for nightclub patrons and 40% for university students. (19)

More specific studies have examined the relationship between marijuana use and driving performance. It is these studies that are more valuable in the context of driving under the influence of marijuana and what specific signs and symptoms are detectable. Such research uses laboratory studies, which investigate the effects of marijuana on skills used in driving; driving simulator studies, which test the effects of marijuana use on driving car simulators designed to replicate actual driving conditions;

and field studies, which explore the degree to which marijuana use is responsible for motor vehicle accidents in the real world. (20)

MARIJUANA AND DRIVING: THE RESEARCH
Laboratory Studies

Laboratory studies that examined the effects of marijuana on skills used while driving have predictably detected impairments in tracking, attention, reaction time, short-term memory, hand-eye coordination, vigilance, time and distance perception, decision making, and concentration. More recent controlled laboratory studies have found that marijuana consumption may impair selective and divided attention tasks, estimation of time, and executive function. (21)

Certain controlled laboratory research has concluded that impairment variations are, not surprisingly, dose-related and typically continue for two to four hours after consumption. (22)(23)(24) Additionally a study conducted by the European Monitoring Centre for Drugs and Addiction concluded that "the acute effect of moderate or higher doses of marijuana impairs the skills related to safe driving and injury risk", particularly "attention, tracking and psychomotor skills" *Id*. This review also determined that the combined effects of marijuana and alcohol on laboratory performance measures are typically greater than the effects of marijuana alone, and act in either an additive or a multiplicative manner. (25)

Driving Simulator Studies

Driving simulator studies have also been administered to determine the relationship between marijuana consumption and driving impairment. A driving simulator is a laboratory based apparatus that simulates real life driving but still lacks realism both in the dynamics of driving a vehicle and in the visual presentation of the road and other traffic. Nonetheless they are able to present simulated dangerous presentations to which the driver must respond.

The early driving simulator studies were not interactive and had as driving scenery a film which afforded the driver little or no control over the presented imagery. Interestingly, these studies showed no significant effects of marijuana on vehicle control. However marijuana did produce the following observed effects, namely:

(i) An increase in decision latency before starting, stopping or overtaking;

(ii) Impaired monitoring of a speedometer; and

(iii) Reduced risk-taking behavior in tasks requiring a decision to overtake a vehicle in the presence of an oncoming car.

Later simulator studies that included more sophisticated and realistic driving dynamics and an interaction between 'scenery' and the driving exercises did show marijuana affected vehicle control. The study by Smiley *et al.* found that marijuana increased lateral position variability, headway variability, and caused the 'driver' to miss more traffic signs. (26) Conversely, marijuana caused the subjects to drive in a more conservative manner as they maintained a longer headway when following another car, declined opportunities to overtake a vehicle in front and when they did pass another vehicle, they began to do so at a greater distance from the approaching vehicle.

Researchers have consistently concluded that there is evidence of dose-dependent impairments in marijuana-affected individuals' ability to control a vehicle in the areas of steering, headway control, speed variability, car following, reaction time and lane positioning. (20) Interestingly it was noted that the levels of impairment detected in simulator studies did not appear to replicate those found in laboratory studies. The researcher speculated that this may be due to the marijuana-affected participants consciously compensating for their impairments. Nonetheless, it should be acknowledged that "even in those who learn to compensate for a drug's impairing effects, substantial impairment in performance can still be observed under conditions of general task performance (i.e. when no contingencies are present to maintain compensated performance." (p. 176)). (25)

Other driving simulator studies have suggested that marijuana use acts in a dose-dependent manner to reduce drivers' average speed and increase their lane position and steering wheel variability and reaction times. (16,17) A separate simulator study determined that marijuana-affected drivers were more likely to report subjectively increased physical effort, discomfort and reduced energy, than were drivers in controlled conditions, again in a dose-dependent manner. (23) However, according to the researchers marijuana use did not appear to have an impact on driver sleepiness or motivation, and driving was not affected by marijuana.

Field Studies

Many field studies have focused on marijuana-affected drivers after their involvement in automobile accidents. The European Monitoring Centre for Drugs and Addiction reviewed 14 separate studies that were undertaken in Australia, Denmark, France, the Netherlands, and the United States between 1993 and 2005. (16)(25) The studies concluded that the rates of marijuana detected in drivers injured in traffic accidents ranged from 3.3% to 26.9% (11.8% on average). Additionally, the combined studies disclosed that, among 23 studies of drivers killed in car accidents in

Australia, Canada, France, Hong Kong, Italy, Spain, Sweden, the United Kingdom and the United States, marijuana was detected in 1.4% to 37% of drivers (11.7% on average). (16)(25)

One of the most comprehensive field studies of marijuana and its effect on driving was performed in The Netherlands and sponsored by the U.S. National Highway Safety Traffic Administration (NHTSA). (29) Three different driving studies were performed for the purposes of this study. The first was conducted on a closed section of a public highway with no traffic; the second on a highway with traffic and the third in urban traffic.

The researchers found that marijuana consumption and driving did cause some deviation of lateral position on the roadway compared to those who did not have any marijuana in their system. Further, the test results indicated that mean speed was somewhat reduced under marijuana as was the headway distance from the lead vehicle in the test in highway traffic (similar to the findings in some simulator studies). For purposes of comparison the study also tested drivers after consumption of alcohol and indicated that drivers under the influence of alcohol had a tendency towards faster driving.

The authors of this study concluded by stating that the effects of cannabis differ qualitatively from those of other depressant drugs, especially alcohol:

Very importantly our city driving study showed that drivers who drank alcohol overestimated their performance quality whereas those who smoked marijuana underestimated it. Perhaps as a consequence, the former invested no special effort for accomplishing the task whereas the latter did, and successfully. This evidence strongly suggests that alcohol encourages risky driving whereas THC encourages greater caution, at least in experiments. *Id.*

The general consensus from most every field study was the very predictable conclusion that the risk of involvement in a traffic accident increased as drivers' THC levels increased, and became significantly greater at higher concentrations of THC. Additionally, researchers also agree that driver culpability studies have suggested that drivers testing positive for marijuana are significantly more likely to be responsible for fatal car crashes than are drug-free drivers. (30)(31)

In conclusion it would appear that these studies, undoubtedly funded by government and educational institutions, have declared the obvious, greater impairment results in greater risk behind the wheel. Not surprisingly, not everyone is in agreement with the studies that have concluded marijuana impairs a driver's ability to safely navigate an automobile.

Summary of Marijuana and its Effects on the Driver

Marijuana and its effects on driving have been studied by different organizations, educational facilities and governments the world over. The majority of these studies concluded that marijuana does impair driving to some degree. Driving impairment by marijuana may include drivers not being able to compensate for standard deviation of lateral position (SDLP, a measure of staying within lane), poorer monitoring of the speedometer under the influence of marijuana, (32) increased decision time when passing, (33) increased time needed to brake when a light suddenly changes, (34) and increased time to respond to a changing light (35)(36) or sudden sound. (37) Drivers were involved in more accidents while on a high dose of marijuana as compared to low doses. (35)

To summarize, laboratory tests and driving studies have shown that marijuana may impair several driving-related skills in a dose-related fashion. However, and importantly, the effects of consuming marijuana on the individual vary more than with alcohol because of tolerance, differences in smoking technique, and different absorptions of THC. Driving and simulator studies show that detrimental effects vary in a doserelated fashion, and are more pronounced with highly automatic driving functions, while more complex tasks that require conscious control are less affected, which is the opposite pattern from that seen with alcohol. These results are in stark contrast with similar studies involving alcohol. Compared to those who have consumed alcohol, the marijuana consumer has an increased level of awareness that they are impaired and as a result tend to compensate more effectively for their impairment by utilizing a variety of behavioral strategies such as driving more slowly, passing less, and leaving more space between themselves and cars in front of them. Combining marijuana with alcohol eliminates the ability to use such strategies effectively however, and results in impairment even at low doses and low levels of alcohol ingestion. While the data and conclusions from studies remain frustratingly inconsistent, there is enough information to suggest that while low concentrations of THC do not increase the rate of accidents, and may even decrease them, concentrations of THC higher than 5 ng/mL are associated with an increased risk of accidents.

CHAPTER 3

Field Sobriety Tests to Detect Marijuana

Once the driver has been detained and there is suspicion of possible intoxication by marijuana, the officer must then utilize tools at his/her disposal to further detect indicators of impairment. Unfortunately for the officer, there is no single test that has been specifically created to detect impairment by marijuana. Therefore the litany of tests available to law enforcement were created to detect possible alcohol impairment, not marijuana intoxication.

NHTSA declares that these tests are "scientifically validated" however, this assertion is not necessarily universally accepted. This contentious issue will be detailed later in the chapter. NHTSA states that based on these tests and on all other evidence gathered from the officer's observations of the driving and physical observations of the driver, the officer must then decide whether there is sufficient probable cause to arrest the driver for DUI.

Following the three standardized field sobriety tests the second task the officer has at his/her option is to administer a preliminary breath test (PBT) to confirm that alcohol is or is not a factor in the perceived impairment. Like the field sobriety tests, the PBT is completely voluntary and the driver may refuse to provide a breath sample. NHTSA does advise the officer that "PBT results cannot be introduced as evidence against the driver in court," although it "can help to corroborate all other evidence and to confirm" the officer's judgment of the driver's impairment. (1) If the PBT renders a low alcohol reading or the absence of alcohol in the driver's system the officer may then refocus his attention on the possibility of the driver being under the influence of marijuana or another type of drug.

Following this second task (and in some cases prior to this second task) the officer must decide whether to arrest the driver for suspicion of DUI. The decision to arrest the driver for DUI is based on all of the evidence the officer has obtained during all three detection phases, namely the observations of the vehicle in motion, face to face observations and the interview of the driver, performance on field sobriety tests and the PBT. According to NHTSA, the DUI "detection process concludes with the arrest decision." (1)

Field sobriety tests have been used throughout the past century in one form or another by police officers to help them assess whether an individual is too impaired to drive an automobile. These tests were initially not very sophisticated and included the smell of alcohol on the breath, the ability of a person to walk a chalk line, and various behavioral signs and symptoms of inebriation. Prior to NHTSA standardizing field sobriety tests in the 1980s, such tests in the United States had little consistency, no standardization, and as a result questionable reliability: "[b]ecause of the inconsistencies in the experimental procedures and approaches used by investigators, few generalizations regarding the influence of alcohol (or drugs) on performance can be advanced." (2)

NHTSA first published SFSTs manuals to be used by law enforcement agencies in field sobriety testing in 1981, with revisions to the originals in 1987, 1992, 1995, 2000, 2002, 2004, 2006, 2009 and 2013. The result was a battery of three standardized field sobriety tests, namely, the horizontal gaze nystagmus (HGN), the walk and turn test, and the one-leg stand. It is universally accepted that the field sobriety testing must be done in accordance with the NHTSA guidelines to be considered relatively reliable. (1) Importantly, and as already mentioned, these tests were designed to detect alcohol impairment and not marijuana impairment. This one fact should never be discounted as alcohol and marijuana impairment are not the same, yet NHTSA treats them similarly.

Standardized Field Sobriety Tests
Horizontal Gaze Nystagmus (HGN)

The technical definition of nystagmus is the rhythmic back and forth oscillation of the eyeball that occurs when there is a disturbance of the vestibular (inner ear) system or the oculomotor control of the eye. There are two major types of eye movements: pendular and jerk. Pendular nystagmus is where the oscillation speed is the same in both directions. Jerk nystagmus is where the eye moves slowly in one direction and then returns rapidly. Most types of nystagmus have the fast and slow phase (jerk nystagmus). Horizontal Gaze Nystagmus (HGN), which is the type of nystagmus used in DUI investigations, is a type of jerk nystagmus with the jerky movement toward the direction of the gaze. (3)

Like most types of nystagmus, HGN is an involuntary motion, meaning the person exhibiting the nystagmus cannot control it or is even aware of it. (4)(5)(6)

Critics of the horizontal gaze nystagmus test for DUI related purposes have argued that alcohol and drugs are not the only potential cause of nystagmus and there are many different causes of nystagmus that have been observed and studied. Syndromes such as influenza, vertigo, epilepsy, measles, syphilis, arteriosclerosis, muscular dystrophy, multiple sclerosis, Korsakoff's Syndrome, brain hemorrhage, streptococcus infections, and other psychogenic disorders all have been shown to produce nystagmus. Additionally, conditions such as hypertension, motion sickness, sunstroke, eyestrain, eye muscle fatigue, glaucoma, and changes in atmospheric pressure may result in gaze nystagmus. (7)

The Horizontal Gaze Nystagmus test in the DUI investigation process involves the officer looking for up to six clues in the driver's eyes. These six clues consist of three maximum clues that can be observed in each eye. According to NHTSA studies if the driver exhibits four or more clues the officer can consider the driver to be under the influence of alcohol.

Administrative Procedures
1. Check for eyeglasses;
2. Verbal instructions;
3. Position stimulus (12-15 INCHES);
4. Equal pupil size and resting nystagmus;
5. Tracking;
6. Lack of smooth pursuit;

7. Distinct and sustained nystagmus at maximum deviation;
8. Onset of nystagmus prior to 45 degrees;
9. Total the clues
10. Check for vertical gaze nystagmus.

The officer must keep the stimulus 12 to 15 inches in front of the driver's face while moving it in a horizontal motion when checking the eyes. The officer is to check the driver's left eye by moving the stimulus to the right. The movement should be done in such a manner that it requires approximately three to four seconds to bring the subject's eye as far as it will go, which is known as the maximum deviation. While moving the stimulus the officer should look at the driver's eyeball and determine whether it is able to pursue smoothly.

After the first eye has been checked for smooth pursuit (or lack of smooth pursuit) the officer should check the same eye for distinct nystagmus at maximum deviation. No selera (white of the eye) will be showing in the corner of the eyeball nearest the ear. It is very important that the officer hold the stimulus at maximum deviation for 2 to 3 seconds.

After checking the eye at maximum deviation the officer should then look for the angle of onset of nystagmus in the same eye. The officer should then move the stimulus back to 0° or straight ahead and then slowly move back towards 45° angle. As the stimulus is moved the officer must watch for the onset of nystagmus. If nystagmus is noted the officer should stop the stimulus and wait for a moment to see if the nystagmus is distinct. If well-defined nystagmus is noted at a specific angle, the officer must note the angle to determine the angle of onset. If nystagmus is not observed, the officer must keep moving the stimulus until nystagmus is noted, or the 45 ° angle is reached. It is important the officer note whether the angle of onset is at or before the 45 ° angle.

Test Interpretation

The Officer should look for three clues of nystagmus in each eye (total of 6 clues).

1. The eye cannot follow a moving object smoothly;
2. Nystagmus is distinct and sustained when the eye is held at maximum deviation for a minimum of four seconds;
3. The angle of onset of nystagmus is prior to 45 degrees.

Vertical Gaze Nystagmus

The Vertical Gaze Nystagmus (VGN) is not officially a "standardized" field sobriety test although NHTSA does group it in with the HGN in their student manual. Therefore all officers are taught how to administer it and the great majority of officers do administer this test immediately following the HGN.

Importantly, this test is not specifically designed to detect marijuana impairment.

Administering the VGN is very much like the HGN except that the stimulus is moving vertical, not horizontal. During the VGN test the officer is looking for jerking in the subject's eyes as the stimulus is moved up and held for approximately four seconds at maximum elevation.

Administrative Procedures
1. Position the stimulus horizontally, about 12-15 inches in front of the suspect's nose;
2. Instruct the suspect to hold the head still, and follow the object with the eyes only;
3. Raise the object until the suspect's eyes are elevated as far as possible;
4. Hold for approximately four seconds;
5. Watch closely for evidence of jerking.

Walk and Turn

The walk and turn test is a "divided attention" test that is designed to determine the subject's balance, listening skills, and ability to follow instructions. In this test the participant stands in a heel-to-toe fashion with arms at their sides while a series of instructions are given by the officer. Following the instructional phase the suspect must then take nine heel-to-toe steps along a line, turn in a prescribed manner, and then take another

FIELD SOBRIETY TESTS TO DETECT MARIJUANA | 35

nine heel-to-toe steps back along the line. All of this must be done while counting the steps aloud and keeping the arms at the sides. The individual is informed not to stop walking until the test is completed.

NHTSA warns the officer that this test requires a "designated straight line and should be conducted on a reasonably dry, hard, level, non-slippery surface." (1) Additionly, the officer is informed in the manual that original research indicated that individuals over the age of 65, and those with back, leg or middle ear problems had difficulty performing the test. Subjects wearing heels more than 2 inches high should be given the opportunity to remove their shoes. *Id.* Over the years however, some of the original instructions and provided information has been deleted from subsequent student manuals.

The walk and turn test has a maximum of eight observable clues in the DUI investigation context. The officer is also trained to observe and note any other noteworthy evidence while the driver is performing the test. Additionally officers are advised to note how many times each of the eight clues appear, even though a clue may only be counted once despite it appearing more than one time.

NHTSA advises that if the driver exhibits at least two clues on the walk and turn test it should be considered evidence that they may be under the influence of alcohol or drugs.

Administrative Procecures

1. **Instructions Stage: Initial Positioning and Verbal Instructions**

   For standardization in the performance of this test, have the suspect assume the heel-to-toe stance by giving the following verbal instructions, accompanied by demonstrations:

   - "Place your left foot on the line" (real or imaginary). Demonstrate.
   - "Place your right foot on the line ahead of the left foot, with heel of right foot against toe of left foot." Demonstrate.
   - "Place your arms down at your sides." Demonstrate.
   - "Maintain this position until I have completed the instructions. Do not start to walk until told to do so."
   - "Do you understand the instructions so far?" (Make sure suspect indicates understanding.)

2. **Demonstrations and Instructions for the Walking Stage**

   Explain the test requirements, using the following verbal instructions, accompanied by demonstrations:

   - "When I tell you to start, take nine heel-to-toe steps, turn, and take nine

heel-to-toe steps back." (Demonstrate 3 heel-to-toe steps.)
- "When you turn, keep the front foot on the line, and turn by taking a series of small steps with the other foot, like this." (Demonstrate).
- "While you are walking, keep your arms at your sides, watch your feet at all times, and count your steps out loud."
- "Once you start walking, don't stop until you have completed the test."
- "Do you understand the instructions?" (Make sure suspect understands.)
- "Begin, and count your first step from the heel-to-toe position as 'One.'"

Test Interpretation

According to NHTSA the Walk and Turn test has a maximum of eight clues that are graded and observed by law enforcement.

Instructional Stage

Two clues apply during the "instructional stage" that occurs while the suspect is standing heel-to-toe and listening to the instructions:
- One clue that is observed by the officer is whether the subject fails to keep balance (i.e. suspect breaks away from the heel-to-toe

stance). Swaying or using arms for balance is not considered a clue at this point; and
- The second clue observed by an officer prior to the walking stage is whether the subject starts walking too soon (i.e. suspect starts walking before you say "begin").

Walking Stage

The remaining six validated clues occur during the walking stage of the test. They are follows:
- Stops walking (i.e. the subject pauses for several seconds).
- Misses heel-to-toe (i.e. more than 1/2 inch gap).
- Steps off the line (i.e. the foot must be entirely off the line).
- Raises the arms while walking (i.e. more than 6 inches).
- Takes the wrong number of steps.
- Turns improperly.

One Leg Stand

The one leg stand test, like the walk and turn field sobriety test, is a divided attention test that is designed to determine the subject's balance, listening skills, and ability to follow instructions. In this test the participant is required to stand on one leg while the other leg is extended in front of the person in a "stiff-leg" manner. This extended foot is to be held approximately six inches above and parallel with the ground. While this is occuring the person is instructed to stare at the elevated foot and count aloud until told to stop, by counting "one thousand and one, one thousand and two, one thousand and three," and so on.

Also, like the walk and turn this test requires a "reasonably dry, hard, level, and non-slippery surface." NHTSA; U.S. Department of Transportation. (1) Further, the officer has knowledge that original research indicated that individuals over the age of 65, and those with back, leg or middle ear problems had difficulty performing the test. Subjects wearing heels more than 2 inches high should be given the opportunity to remove their shoes. *Id.*

Administrative Procecures

Per NHTSA, the officer is instructed to give the test as follows:

- Tell suspect to stand with feet together and arms down at the sides.
- Tell suspect to maintain that position while you give the instructions; emphasize that they should not try to perform the test until you say to "begin."
- Ask suspect if they understand.
- Tell suspect that when you say to "begin" they must raise their leg in a stiff-leg manner,

and hold the foot approximately six inches off the ground, with the toe pointed forward so that the foot is parallel with the ground.
- Demonstrate the proper one-legged stance.
- Tell suspect that they must keep the arms at the sides and must keep looking directly at the elevated foot, while counting in the following fashion: "one thousand and one, one thousand and two, one thousand and three," and so on until told to stop.
- Ask the suspect if he or she understands.
- Tell the suspect to "begin."

The officer is also given the following instruction:
- It is important that this test last for thirty seconds. You must keep track of the time. If the suspect counts slowly, you will tell him or her to stop when thirty actual seconds have gone by, even if, for example, the suspect has only counted to "one thousand and twenty."

Test Interpretation

The One Leg Stand has four clues of impairment:
- Sways while balancing (side to side or back to front).
- Uses arms to balance (i.e., more than 6 inches).
- Hopping.
- Puts foot down.

General Criticisms of SFSTs

Proponents of these studies conclude that the standardization of FSTs has produced more accurate and reliable determination of possible DUI drivers. However, there have been many critics.

Critics of the NHTSA backed studies state that they are not peer-reviewed, thereby skipping an important review of the study itself. The peer review process enables other scientists to critique the experimental method and conclusions reached by the article's author(s). Research within these studies and their design and criterion must also meet generally acceptable scientific standards. To wit, a study such as the ones conducted to test SFSTs must include a control group and eliminate variables that can distort results. The tests relied on by NHTSA fail to do this, according to NHTSA's critics.

Another criticism of the SFSTs is that they cannot be considered reliable until the mean and standard deviation of normal performance is established. Interestingly no controlled (NHTSA sponsored) studies have been completed to determine the normal range of SFST performance for sober individuals. However, there is one study that examined the concept that normal, sober individuals may be considered impaired based either on field sobriety tests or normal abilities tests. In the study, 21 sober participants (between

42 | THE MARIJUANA DUI HANDBOOK

21-55 years of age, no known physical disabilities, and of normal weight) were videotaped while performing field sobriety tests and fourteen police officers were assigned to view their performance. (8)

After examining the performances, the officers in the study were asked to determine if the participant was impaired. Forty-six percent of the officers declared that a sober participant in the study had "too much to drink" based on the FST performance. In this study, only 3 participants were determined to be sober by all officers, although every one of the participants was in fact, sober. *Id.*

Other arguments against the validity of the SFSTs come from those who believe that these tests do not and cannot prove that the subject was driving under the influence. Importantly no individual from NHTSA, DOT, or the NHTSA-commissioned researchers have ever claimed that the SFSTs are direct indicators of actual driving impairment. Stuster and Burns recognized the limitations and stated:

"[d]riving a motor vehicle is a very complex activity that involves a wide variety of tasks and operator capabilities. It is unlikely that complex human performance, such as that required to safely drive an automobile, can be measured at roadside. The constraints imposed by roadside testing conditions were recognized by the developers of NHTSA's

SFST battery. As a consequence, they pursued the development of tests that would provide statistically valid and reliable indications of a driver's BAC, rather than indications of driving impairment. (9)

Another study declared that "even valid, behavioral tests are likely to be poor predictors either of actual behind-the-wheel driving." (10)

Critics of the standardized field sobriety tests also included some within law enforcement. The California Highway Patrol criticizes the SFSTs and its Training Manual states that the "HGN is not a psychophysical test. The clues associated with HGN are not designed to be considered 'signs of impairment.'" (11) Critics have argued that the SFSTs are not nearly as reliable as the studies allege and that officers do not always comply with the SFST procedures, the HGN measurement is not always exact, the reliability claims of the studies were misleading, the officers in the studies were more experienced than average (and given a refresher course immediately prior to testing), and so on. These critics may have a point as it is difficult to accurately emulate these tests in the real world. (12) Further, critics have argued that very few of the SFSTs are conducted in exact accordance with NHTSA rules. (13) To that end, NHTSA states that "[i]f any one of the standardized field sobriety test elements is changed, the validity is compromised." (1)

Non-Standardized Field Sobriety Tests

While the standardized field sobriety tests are now common place and regularly practiced by law enforcement when investigating a possible DUI driver, the non-standardized field sobriety tests are still commonly used by law enforcement. Obviously the validity of these tests remain questionable because of the lack of standardization and consistency.

Romberg Test

Of all the non-standardized field sobriety tests, the best known and most commonly used is the Romberg Balance Test. A German ear specialist by the name of Moritz Heinrich Romberg developed a balance assessment test in 1853 that could be used to diagnose diseases. This test is known as the "Romberg Test" and is widely used as a non-specific test of neurological or inner ear dysfunction. The Romberg Test has been modified for use by police officers in the performance of Field Sobriety Tests, although this test is not a standardized Field Sobriety Test.

The Romberg Test is a neurological test to determine whether a subject can keep a steady standing position with the eyes closed. The basic test requires an individual to stand with his feet together, hands at his side, head tilted back, and eyes closed. The basic test has developed into several different variations. These different versions are commonly referred to as the "Sharpened" and the "Modified Position of Attention" Romberg Tests.

While there have been no studies validating the Romberg test in the DUI context, a number of studies have been conducted concluding that the Romberg Test when performed in the law enforcement environment is unreliable. (14) Additionally, studies have found that the increased sway found in testing can relate to things other than alcohol or drug intoxication, such as weight, age, physical condition, exercise, sleep loss, elevated temperatures, and antihistamines. (15)

Administrative Procecures

<u>Step One</u>

Instruction Stage and Initial Positioning

Explain the initial instructions in the following manner:

- When told to do so, stand with your heels and toes together, your arms down at your side (demonstrate)
- Close your eyes, tilt your head backwards (demonstrate) and listen to the remainder of the instructions
- Do you understand? (Make sure the subject indicates that he or she understands; if not, repeat the instructions and note the impaired cognitive thought process)
- Go ahead, take the initial position

Step Two

Instruction, Balancing and Counting Stage

While the subject is balancing in the initial explain the following:

- While you are balancing, you must determine when 30 seconds have elapsed from the time you are told to begin
- When you believe that 30 seconds has elapsed, tilt your head down and look straight ahead. You may count silently to yourself if you wish
- Do you understand? (Make sure the subject indicates that he or she understands, if not, repeat the instructions and note the impaired cognitive thought processes).

While the driver is mentally calculating when 30 seconds have elapsed, utilize a stopwatch or the second hand of a wristwatch to determine when the time has actually elapsed. If the subject is intoxicated on CNS depressants, their determination of 30 seconds will be longer. If they are intoxicated on a CNS stimulant, their determination of 30 seconds will be shorter than the actual 30 second interval.

Test Interpretation

<u>Step Three</u>

Scoring Modified Romberg Test

Score one point for each of the following items:
- Required additional instructions during the test;
- Opened eyes during the test;
- Failed to keep heels together during the test;
- Failed to keep head tilted back;
- Swayed more than 4 inches off center, side to side or front to back. A figure 8 motion may also be observed;
- More than 10 second difference in time;
- Unable to do the test. If the subject is in danger of falling over or, for whatever reason, is not able to accomplish the test, score a total of 7 points.
- The modified Romberg Test requires a hard, dry, level, non-slip surface. Conditions must be such that the subject will not endanger themselves. Individuals who have a painful neck, back or leg ailments or other injuries, should not attempt this test.

Finger to Nose

Another commonly used non-standardized field sobriety test is the finger to nose test. This test is a basic test that requires the subject to close his eyes and then touch the tip of his nose with the tip of his index finger, alternating hands. NHTSA research and studies revealed that the finger to nose test, along with the Romberg Test, only indicated the presence of alcohol or drugs, and "did not increase the predictive ability of testing." (16)

Alphabet, Count Down, and Finger Count Tests

Other non-standardized field sobriety tests that are often used are the alphabet recitation, a numerical count down, and finger count tests. The alphabet test requires the subject to recite part of the alphabet (e.g., starting at a letter other than A and stopping at a letter other than Z). The countdown test simply requires the subject to count aloud numbers in reverse, from highest to lowest, for example, counting backwards from 50 to 30. The finger count test requires the subject to touch the tip of the thumb to the tip of each finger on the same hand in a particular order while counting (e.g., "one, two, three, four—four, three, two, one).

These tests were considered in the initial NHTSA study in 1977 but were discarded and therefore not selected as accurate indicators of alcohol or drug impairment. The Standardized Field Sobriety Test (SFST) Student Manual warns that these techniques are not as reliable as the SFST tests and "do not replace the SFST." (1)

Procedures for the Finger Count Test

<u>Step One</u>

Instruction State and Demonstration

Explain, in the following manner, the instructions to be followed by the subject:

- Tell the subject to stand or sit comfortably;
- Using either hand, count out loud while touching the tip of each finger with the tip of the finger. You must count exactly like this (demonstrate how the thumb is used to count on the tip of each finger and further, how the subject must count out loud) (1-2-3-4—4-3-2-1)
- Do this series three times
- Do you understand? (make sure the subject indicates that he or she understands; if not, repeat the instructions and note the impaired cognitive thought processes)
- Begin

<u>Step Two</u>

Performance

Observe the subject carefully to determine whether he or she performs the test as instructed and demonstrated

Step Three
Scoring Finger Count Test
- Required additional instruction during testing
- Used a hand other than the one designated
- Missed touching all the proper fingers
- Counted incorrectly
- Was unable to accomplish the test

There are very few requirements for the Finger Count test. It can be used in place of the modified Romberg or One Leg Stand Tests when the subject complains of physical injuries or illnesses. An individual who has difficulty moving their fingers or is missing fingers should not attempt this test.

MARIJUANA AND FIELD SOBRIETY TESTS
Studies and Research

Field sobriety testing in the context of driving under the influence has been studied, complimented and criticized endlessly throughout the years. However, the study of field sobriety testing specific to marijuana impairment has been poor. Very few studies have been undertaken that have focused on the standardized field sobriety tests as their relationship to marijuana impairment. The few studies that have occurred have usually grouped in marijuana with other drugs (including alcohol), which have lead to rather vague results when it comes to marijuana. Perhaps the problem is that the standardized field sobriety tests were studied for alcohol only, and were never designed to detect marijuana impairment.

One of the more thorough studies that focused on marijuana and field sobriety testing occurred in Victoria, Australia. (17) According to the study the goal of the research "was to assess whether the SFSTs provide a sensitive measure of impairment following the consumption of a drug other than alcohol: delta-9-tetrahydrocannabinol (THC or cannabis)." Further, they openly admitted in their study that

> [T]he SFST battery was specifically developed to test for alcohol intoxication and no empirical research has been performed to assess whether the SFSTs provide a sensitive measure of impairment following the consumption of a drug other than alcohol. Such research is required to determine whether the SFSTs are suitable for this purpose.

The study was clinically controlled and the subjects tested were under the influence of only THC at the time of testing. Further, the study stated that it is "difficult to ascertain whether the percentages of THC administered in the present study are similar to the percentage of THC contained in commonly obtained street cannabis as available data does not reveal the strength of seized cannabis."

The study concluded that the consumption of THC does impair performance on the SFSTs. Not surprisingly the study also found that the "higher the content of THC consumed, the greater the number of participants that were classified as impaired."

Horizontal Gaze Nystagmus

The Australian study first examined the HGN test with individuals who had consumed marijuana and had TCH active in their system. Using the standard scoring procedure for the SFSTs, the researchers determined that the primary indicator of impairment during the HGN test was the lack of smooth pursuit, the first of the three clues (in each eye) to be examined in this test. Further, the study stated that the lack of smooth pursuit was significantly related to the levels of THC in the subjects blood.

Although the study declared that lack of smooth pursuit was the primary indicator of impairment by THC during the HGN test, it was not the single best HGN related indicator of marijuana impairment. According to the study head movements or jerks (HMJ) was the most commonly observed indicator in this test. This study recommended that HMJ be included in the HGN testing of marijuana impaired individuals as it was detected at both low and high levels of THC. However, and importantly, HMJ is not a "clue" in the HGN SFST, so this finding has yet to be adopted into any North American sobriety testing as a clue to determine marijuana impairment.

Walk and Turn

The researchers in the Australian study then turned their attention to the walk and turn test and marijuana impairment. They noted that there were two signs in this particular test that were observed at all times in the subjects tested, specifically the subjects consistently had poor balance and that arms were used for balance. The study thus concluded that in both low and high dose conditions, balance was significantly impaired. They further stated that the "findings suggest that the administration of THC impairs the ability to maintain balance, as well as to focus attention." Equally important was the finding that three signs (or clues) from the walk and turn test were found to be unrelated to the level of THC at all administrations of this test. These three clues are: missing heel to toe, improper turn, and the incorrect number of steps. Based on this finding the researchers suggested that these three clues may result in a high incidence of "false positives" and therefore they recommended that further research be conducted to "determine whether such signs should be excluded from the SFST scoring procedures." (17)

One Leg Stand

Of the three standardized field sobriety tests reviewed in this study the One Leg Stand was thought to be the best indicator of impairment associated with the administration of THC. The study noted that "[i]t has previously been argued that the One Leg Stand may be too sensitive for determining drug use and that many individuals may not have very good balance even when they are not under the influence of drugs." Despite these fears, which had been previously published, this study believed the inclusion of the one leg stand is important for determining marijuana impairment. The researchers believed the value of the one leg stand would be to use it in conjunction with both the horizontal gaze nystagmus and the walk and turn but to give the one leg stand more weight and consideration.

CHAPTER 4

Drug Recognition Experts (DRE)

History and Development

A drug recognition expert or drug recognition evaluator (DRE) is a police officer who is trained to recognize impairment in drivers who are under the influence of drugs other than, or in addition to, alcohol. The International Association of Chiefs of Police (IACP) coordinates the International Drug Evaluation and Classification (DEC) Program with support from the National Highway Traffic Safety Administration (NHTSA) of the U.S. Department of Transportation. The DRE process is also being utilized by law enforcement in Canada and Australia, in addition to the United States.

The Los Angeles Police Department (LAPD) originated the DRE program in the early 1970s after LAPD officers noticed that many of the individuals arrested for driving under the influence had very low or zero blood alcohol concentrations. The officers suspected that the arrestees were under the influence of drugs but lacked the knowledge and skills to support their suspicions. As a result two LAPD sergeants collaborated with various medical doctors, research psychologists, and other medical professionals to develop a simple, standardized procedure for recognizing drug influence and impairment. Their efforts culminated in the development of a multi-step protocol and the first DRE program. The LAPD formally recognized the program in 1979. (1)

In the early 1980s NHTSA started to take notice of the LAPD DRE. The two agencies worked together to develop a standardized DRE protocol, which led to the development of the DEC Program. During the ensuing years, NHTSA and various other agencies and research groups examined the DEC program and their studies attempted to demonstrate that a properly trained DRE can successfully identify drug impairment and accurately determine the category of drugs causing such impairment. The success of a DRE examination is naturally up for debate, depending on who you ask.

The DRE protocol is, according to the literature, a

standardized and systematic method of examining a Driving Under the Influence of Drugs (DUID) suspect to determine whether or not he is impaired and, if so, whether the impairment relates to drugs or a medical condition. The advocates of the DRE process believe that the program is designed to be systematic because it is based on a set of observable signs and symptoms that are known, according to the program, to be reliable indicators of drug impairment.

The concept of the DRE evaluation is that a conclusion of drug impairment is not based on one particular element but instead on the totality of facts that emerge from the evaluation. Like the SFST program from NHTSA, the DRE evaluation is standardized because it is supposed to be conducted the same way, by every drug recognition expert, for every suspect whenever possible. Standardization, in theory, is important because it makes the officers better observers, helps to avoid errors, and promotes professionalism. Naturally this assumes that every DRE evaluation is done in exact accordance with the protocol outlined below.

Arguments against validating drug recognition experts are many and begin with the simple fact that DREs are not medically trained professionals and therefore cannot render a judgment of an individual's impairment based on the criterion provided. Further, the DRE program is usually taught by other law enforcement personnel and not by medical professionals.

The 12-Step DRE Protocol

The DREs utilize a 12-step process in reviewing potential drivers under the influence of drugs. The 12-step process usually requires approximately 30-45 minutes to complete, however, the evaluation can take longer depending on the drug ingested. These twelve steps include the following:

1. *Breath Alcohol Test:* The arresting officer reviews the subject's breath alcohol concentration (BAC) test results and determines if the subject's apparent impairment is consistent with the subject's BAC. If so, the officer will not normally call a DRE. If the impairment is not explained by the BAC, the officer requests a DRE evaluation.

2. *Interview of the Arresting Officer:* The DRE begins the investigation by reviewing the BAC test results and discussing the circumstances of the arrest with the arresting officer, if he was not the arresting officer. The DRE asks about the subject's behavior, appearance, and driving. The DRE also asks if the subject made any statements regarding drug use and if the arresting officer(s) found any other relevant evidence consistent with drug use.

3. *Preliminary Examination and First Pulse:* The DRE conducts a preliminary examination to determine whether the subject may be suffering from an injury or other condition unrelated to drugs.

DRUG RECOGNITION EXPERTS (DRE) | 59

Accordingly, the DRE asks the subject a series of standard questions relating to the subject's health and recent ingestion of food, alcohol and drugs, including prescribed medications. The DRE observes the subject's attitude, coordination, speech, breath and face. The DRE also determines if the subject's pupils are of equal size and if the subject's eyes can follow a moving stimulus and track equally. The DRE also looks for horizontal gaze nystagmus (HGN) and takes the subject's pulse for the first of three times. The DRE takes each subject's pulse three times to account for nervousness, check for consistency and determine if the subject is getting worse or better. If the DRE believes that the subject may be suffering from a significant medical condition, the DRE will seek medical assistance immediately. If the DRE believes that the subject's condition is drug-related, the evaluation continues.

4. *Eye Examination:* The DRE examines the subject for HGN, vertical gaze nystagmus (VGN) and for a lack of ocular convergence. A subject lacks convergence if his eyes are unable to converge toward the bridge of his nose when a stimulus is moved inward. Depressants, inhalants, and dissociative anesthetics, the so-called "DID drugs", may cause HGN. In addition, the DID drugs may cause VGN when taken in higher doses for that individual.

DID drugs, as well as cannabis (marijuana), may also cause a lack of convergence.

5. *Divided Attention Psychophysical Tests:* The DRE administers four psychophysical tests: the Romberg Balance, the Walk and Turn, the One Leg Stand, and the Finger to Nose tests. The DRE can accurately determine if a subject's psychomotor and/or divided attention skills are impaired by administering these tests.

6. *Vital Signs and Second Pulse:* The DRE takes the subject's blood pressure, temperature and pulse. Some drug categories may elevate the vital signs. Others may lower them. Vital signs provide valuable evidence of the presence and influence of a variety of drugs.

7. *Dark Room Examinations:* The DRE estimates the subject's pupil sizes under three different lighting conditions with a measuring device called a pupilometer. The device will assist the DRE in determining whether the subject's pupils are dilated, constricted, or normal. Some drugs increase pupil size (dilate), while others may decrease (constrict) pupil size. The DRE also checks for the eyes' reaction to light. Certain drugs may slow the eyes' reaction to light. Finally, the DRE examines the subject's nasal and oral cavities for signs of drug ingestion.

8. *Examination for Muscle Tone:* The DRE examines

the subject's skeletal muscle tone. Certain categories of drugs may cause the muscles to become rigid. Other categories may cause the muscles to become very loose and flaccid.

9. *Check for Injection Sites and Third Pulse:* The DRE examines the subject for injection sites, which may indicate recent use of certain types of drugs. The DRE also takes the subject's pulse for the third and final time.

10. *Subject's Statements and Other Observations:* The DRE typically reads *Miranda*, if not done so previously, and asks the subject a series of questions regarding the subject's drug use.

11. *Analysis and Opinions of the Evaluator:* Based on the totality of the evaluation, the DRE forms an opinion as to whether or not the subject is impaired. If the DRE determines that the subject is impaired, the DRE will indicate what category or categories of drugs may have contributed to the subject's impairment. The DRE bases these conclusions on his training and experience and the DRE Drug Symptomatology Matrix. While DREs use the drug matrix, they also rely heavily on their general training and experience.

12. *Toxicological Examination:* After completing the evaluation, the DRE normally requests a urine, blood and/or saliva sample from the subject for a toxicology lab analysis.

Drug Categories Evaluated by a DRE

The DRE categorization process is premised on the belief championed by physicians that different types of drugs affect people differently. Accordingly drugs may be categorized or classified corresponding to certain shared symptomatologies or effects, and as a result these drugs are divided into one of seven categories: Central Nervous System (CNS) Depressants, CNS Stimulants, Hallucinogens, Phencyclidine (PCP) and its analogs, Narcotic Analgesics, Inhalants, and Cannabis. It is believed that drugs from each of these seven categories can possibly affect a person's central nervous system and impair a person's normal faculties, and in the DUI field, affect a person's ability to safely operate a motor vehicle.

1. *Central Nervous System (CNS) Depressants:* CNS Depressants slow down the operations of the brain and the body. Examples include alcohol, barbiturates, anti-anxiety tranquilizers (e.g. Valium, Librium, Xanax, Prozac, Thorazine), GHB (Gamma Hydroxybutyrate), Rohypnol and many other anti-depressants (e.g., Zoloft, Paxil).

2. *CNS Stimulants:* CNS Stimulants accelerate the heart rate and elevate the blood pressure and "speed-up" or over-stimulate the body and include Cocaine, "Crack", Amphetamines and Methamphetamine.

3. *Hallucinogens:* Hallucinogens cause the user to

perceive things differently than they actually are. Examples include LSD, Peyote, Psilocybin and MDMA (Ecstasy).
4. *Dissociative Anesthetics:* Dissociative Anesthetics are drugs that inhibit pain by cutting off or dissociating the brain's perception of the pain. PCP and its analogs are examples of Dissociative Anesthetics.
5. *Narcotic Analgesics:* Narcotic analgesic relieves pain, induce euphoria and create mood changes in the user. Examples include Opium, Codeine, Heroin, Demerol, Darvon, Morphine, Methadone, Vicodin and OxyContin.
6. *Inhalants:* Inhalants include a wide variety of breathable substances that produce mind-altering results and effects. Examples of inhalants include Toluene, plastic cement, paint, gasoline, paint thinners, hair sprays and various anesthetic gases.
7. *Cannabis:* Cannabis (marijuana) is a popular drug consumed prior to driving. The active ingredient in cannabis is delta-9 tetrahydrocannabinol, or THC. This category includes cannabinoids and synthetics like Dronabinol.

The Tools of the Trade: DRE equipment

A DRE utilizes the following equipment in conducting a drug influence evaluation:
- Pupillometer: a small, approximately 3 inch by 5 inch card (approximately 7 to 12 cm),

that is usually plastic, that displays dark circles ranging in half-millimeter gradations from 1.0 millimeters to 9.0 millimeters.
- Sphygmomanometer: a manual, aneroid blood pressure cuff consisting of a pumping bulb, a screw valve, an analog gauge, and a bladder.
- Stethoscope: single or double diaphragm, double tubed.
- Thermometer: oral, digital, with disposable covers.
- Penlight: low power, medical style.
- Magnifying light: generally five to ten magnification power, similar to those used by stamp collectors and model builders.
- Pen or Pencil: used as a stylus to conduct eye movement examinations.
- Evidence containers: for blood or urine.
- Protective gloves, latex and/or rubber.

In addition, DREs may utilize a specialized, short distance, instant camera to take photos of injection marks, nasal and oral cavities, and of other evidence. DREs may also utilize various type of breath testing equipment, including preliminary breath testers.

Drug Recognition Expert (DRE) Training

The International Association of Chiefs of Police (IACP) coordinates the International Drug Evaluation and Classification (DEC) Program with support from the National Highway Traffic Safety Administration (NHTSA) of the U.S. Department of Transportation. According to the American Prosecutors Research Institute (APRI) "[m]any police departments handpick all DRE candidates." (2)

Training for a drug recognition expert can only be undertaken once the law enforcement officer has completed basic training and is certified in the NHTSA standardized field sobriety testing. Once these formalities are met the officer is permitted to begin the three phase Drug Evaluation and Classification (DEC) Program.

Phase One: The 16-hour DRE Pre-school includes an overview of the DRE evaluation procedures, the seven drug categories, eye examinations and proficiency in conducting the SFSTs.

Phase Two: The 56-hour DRE School includes an overview of the drug evaluation procedures, expanded sessions on each drug category, drug combinations, examination of vital signs, case preparation, courtroom testimony, and Curriculum Vitae (C.V.) preparation. At the conclusion of the 7-days of training, the officer must successfully complete a written examination before moving to the third and final phase of training.

Phase Three: During this phase the candidate must complete a minimum of 12 drug evaluations under the supervision of a trained DRE instructor. Of those 12 evaluations, the officer must identify an individual under the influence of at least three of the seven drug categories and obtain a minimum 75% toxicological corroboration rate. The officer must then pass a final knowledge examination and be approved by two DRE instructors before being certified as a certified DRE.

Further, the instruction and internship period where the DRE conducts actual drug evaluations is under the tutelage of a certified DRE instructor. APRI is silent regarding whether the instructor must be medically trained or simply a law enforcement officer. This silence confirms what is readily known, that DRE instructors do not necessarily have any medical training. This fact is concerning because, as APRI points out, "[b]ecause of their enhanced training, DREs are better equipped than other officers to identify medical impairments." *Id.* at 3

This statement may be correct but does not address how competent this medical training actually is and further, if the DRE training program is considered "medical training."

The three distinct phases of DRE training are then divided into thirteen individual criterion which eventually results in certification by the IACP. http://www.ndaa.org The criteria is as follows:

1. Standardized Field Sobriety Test (SFST) training

2. DRE preliminary training
3. DRE School
4. DRE School Classroom Examination
5. Minimum number of evaluations
6. Minimum number of drug categories observed
7. Toxicological corroboration
8. "Rolling" log reviewed
9. Resume reviewed
10. Certification final examination
11. Endorsement by an instructor
12. Endorsement by a second instructor
13. Certification by the International Association of Chiefs of Police.

Criterion One: Standardized Field Sobriety Test (SFST) Training

Although there are a number of formats for this first phase of DRE training, the usual format consists of two days of training in the proper administration and interpretation of the standardized field sobriety test battery. This segment is primarily skill-oriented. Students practice administering the SFST on volunteers who consume alcohol. In order to complete this phase, students must successfully pass both a written examination and a proficiency test. SFST training is a "stand-alone" course, in that most officers who complete SFST training never continue into DRE training. This phase of the training may also include an introductory overview of the drugs that impair driving.

Criterion Two: DRE Preliminary Training
Following the SFST training, officers that will continue with DRE training must successfully complete a two day DRE preliminary training course. This course expands upon the officers' SFST skills, provides an overview of the DRE procedures, and provides an overview of the effects of the drugs of abuse. In this segment, officers are also taught to properly administer the vital signs examinations that are conducted in a DRE evaluation. Some agencies combine the SFST and DRE preliminary training into a unified four-day course. The LAPD also conducts an accelerated ten-day format that combines SFST training, DRE Preliminary Training, and the DRE course itself into one unified ten-day training event.

Criterion Three: DRE School
This segment of the training consists of seven classroom days of intensive training. There are 31 separate segments to the course. Some of the specific segments are: the physiology of the drugs of abuse, the development and effectiveness of the DRE procedures, vital signs examinations, eye

examinations, courtroom testimony, and drug combinations. Each of the seven categories of drugs are covered in depth. Commonly abused substances, methods of administration, and the duration of effects are extensively covered. Students view video-tapes of individuals under the influence of the various categories, and participate in many interpretative exercises. Students also practice the administration of the DRE procedure while under the direct supervision of DRE instructors. Students are tested throughout this phase. Under the guidelines established for DRE training by the International Association of Chiefs of Police, students cannot "test-out" of any of the segments of the course, and must make-up any missed classes.

Criterion Four: DRE School Examination
At the conclusion of the DRE school, students take a comprehensive written objective examination. Eighty percent is the minimum passing score.

Criterion Five: Minimum number of evaluations
This stage begins the certification phase of DRE training. Much like an internship, the student must demonstrate his or her proficiency in properly conducting and interpreting DRE evaluations that are given to actual suspects. The minimum national

standards require the DRE student to conduct 12 full drug evaluations. Many agencies, including the LAPD, require 15 evaluations. Some of the required evaluations may include medical rule-outs, and evaluations in which no drug influence was determined by the DRE student. All of the evaluations during this phase must be conducted under the direct supervision of a DRE instructor.

Criterion Six: Minimum number of drug categories observed

Student DREs must evaluate individuals who are under the influence of at least three of the seven categories of drugs. (The LAPD and many other agencies require four drug categories.) The student DRE must correctly conduct the evaluations, and must reach appropriate conclusions. All three drug categories must be supported by toxicology.

Criterion Seven: Toxicological corroboration

During certification, student DREs must submit a minimum of nine physical specimens, blood or urine, to a laboratory for analysis. The laboratory analysis is compared to the student DRE's opinion as to the type of drug influencing the individual. The student must achieve a 75% laboratory confirmation rate. This means that at least 75% of the samples submitted to the laboratory must result in the laboratory finding a drug belonging to the category the student DRE identified.[43] A 75% standard does not mean that the student can be wrong 25% of the time. A student's opinion must always be supported by the individual's presenting signs and symptoms. It does allow, however, for those instances in which the laboratory is not able to detect the type of drug the student DRE had identified.

Criterion Eight: "Rolling" log reviewed

All DREs must maintain a log of all the evaluations, including toxicological results, they have conducted. This log is then submitted to a DRE instructor for review. This log is critical in establishing the DRE's expertise in court, as in documenting DRE experience for recertification.

Criterion Nine: Resume reviewed

Each DRE must maintain an up-to-date resume. This resume should list the training the DRE has received, additional readings, court qualifications, formal education, publications, and other relevant experiences. As is the case with the "rolling" log, the primary purpose of the resume is to enhance the credibility and consistency of the DRE when testifying in court. This resume must be presented for review by a DRE instructor. A copy of the resume is maintained by an agency's DRE coordinator.

Criterion Ten: Certification Final Examination

This comprehensive written examination is given when the student DRE is approaching the conclusion of certification training. This examination, which typically takes from between three and six hours, requires the student DRE to articulate the signs and symptoms of the various drugs, including numerous drug combinations. The examination is scored on a pass-fail basis by a DRE instructor. This examination is similar in concept to examinations given in graduate school that require the student to demonstrate knowledge of all aspects of drug effects.

Criterion Eleven: Endorsement by an instructor

The student DRE is required to secure in writing the recommendation of a DRE instructor stating that the student should be awarded certification. Only DRE instructors that have actually supervised the student DRE may endorse the student.

Criterion Twelve: Endorsement by a second instructor

This step requires the written endorsement of a second DRE instructor.

Criterion Thirteen: Certification by the International Association of Chiefs of Police.

Once criteria one through twelve have been completed, the student DRE submits all the required documentation to the agency's DRE coordinator. After reviewing the completed package, the agency coordinator approves and submits certification documents to the International Association of Chiefs of Police (IACP) through a state coordinator. A tracking number is assigned to the DRE, and certificates are issued to the new DRE by the IACP. Certification is for a two year period.

Recertification and Continuing Education

In order to maintain certification, the DRE must attend a minimum of eight hours of continuing education training each two years. Many agencies require a minimum of eight hours of continuing education annually. Typically, the continuing education includes reviewing and practicing the DRE procedures, case law, toxicological issues, and an update on new drugs and drug use trends. The DRE must also have conducted a minimum of four drug influence evaluations during this period, one of which is directly supervised by a DRE instructor. The IACP has also adopted continuing education requirements for DRE instructors.

Presently 45 states in the US, plus the District of Columbia, are participating in the program. These states are: Alaska, Arizona, Arkansas, California, Colorado, Delaware, Florida, Georgia, Hawaii, Idaho, Illinois, Indiana, Iowa, Kansas, Kentucky, Louisiana, Maine, Maryland, Massachusetts, Minnesota, Mississippi, Missouri, Montana, Nebraska, Nevada, New Hampshire, New Jersey, New Mexico, New York, North Carolina, North Dakota, South Dakota, Oklahoma, Oregon, Pennsylvania, Rhode Island, South Carolina, Tennessee, Texas, Utah, Vermont, Virginia, Washington, Wisconsin, and Wyoming.

DRE Testimony

In certain cases when a DRE has performed his duties he may be asked by the prosecuting attorney to testify as a "technical" expert at trial. Although a DRE is not a doctor, pharmacologist, or toxicologist, he does have specialized knowledge that will assist the trier-of-fact to understand the evidence.

According to the National District Attorneys Association a DRE testifies for three specific purposes. http://www.ndaa.org

> *First,* the DRE establishes that the driver's impairment is caused by a drug or drugs other than or in addition to alcohol, and rules out a medical condition or medical emergency;
>
> *Second,* the DRE identifies and notes the category

of drug consumed by the suspect, which is helpful to the toxicology laboratory in determining which substances to test for. The DRE does not identify a specific drug, such as cocaine, but rather the general category of drugs (e.g., in the case of cocaine, a central nervous system stimulant). Just as the officer is not required to determine the type of alcohol or the brand of beer a suspect consumed in order to offer an opinion that an individual is driving under the influence of alcohol, the DRE is not required to identify the specific drug.

Third, at trial, the DRE will testify to all the signs and symptoms of impairment he or she observed and may be allowed to offer an opinion that the impairment is consistent with the drugs verified by the chemical test. Regardless of whether the DRE is allowed to offer such an opinion, the prosecutor will likely call on a toxicologist to further explain the connection between the signs of impairment observed by the DRE and the drug found by the toxicology lab.

In the drugged-driving case, there must be evidence that a drug or combination of drugs caused the impairment. Therefore, testimony on the signs and symptoms of drug impairment is critical to the fact finder's ability to determine (1) the person was impaired **and** (2) the impairment was the result of a substance other than, or in addition to, alcohol.

Indicators Consistent With Marijuana

Major Indicators	Cannabis
HGN	None
VGN	None
Lack of Convergence	Present
Pupil Size	Dilated(6)
Reaction to Light	Normal
Pulse Rate	Up
Blood Pressure	Up
Body Temp.	Normal
Duration of Effects	2-3 hours exhibits effects (Impairment may last up to 24 hours without awareness of effect)
Usual methods of Admin.	Smoked Oral
Overdose Signs	Fatigue Paranoia

NOTES: These indicators are those most consistent with the category, keep in mind that there may be variations due to individual reaction, dose taken and drug interactions.

Normal ranges
Pulse: 60-90 beats per minute
Pupil size: 2.5 – 5.0 (Room Light); 5.0 – 8.5 (Near Total Darkness); 2.0 – 4.5 (Direct Light)
Blood pressure: 120-140 Systolic; 70-90 Diastolic
Body temperature: 98.6 +/- 1.0 degree

CHAPTER 5

Blood Testing for Marijuana

Determining whether a driver is under the influence of drugs can be surmised from physical observations of the driver, field sobriety tests, and an examination from a drug recognition expert (DRE). However, the only precise way to determine exactly what drugs (and the amount) are in the driver's system is from a blood test. This is critical in cases involving marijuana because impairment is often dose dependent.

The gathering of chemical evidence must meet certain legal requirements in order to be accepted in a court of law. These requirements focus on both statutory and regulatory guidelines for the types of test specimens as well as the testing procedures. If such guidelines are not followed by law enforcement or medical personal the chemical evidence may not be admissible in court. Additionally, if a particular testing device or machine has not been certified for use by the State where the incident occurred, any results obtained should be suppressed. As a result it is important for law enforcement to be familiar with the regulatory guidelines set down by the State's Department of Health or other appropriate regulatory agency.

State and other regulations generally govern all forms of chemical testing for blood alcohol content. The manner of test, the procedures by which tests are given, the qualifications of individuals performing those tests and even the methods of reporting the test results may be governed by statute or regulation.

In states where blood evidence is collected and used as evidence against the driver the arresting officer typically requests the driver to submit to a blood draw. If the driver agrees, the blood is drawn and then sent to an approved state forensic laboratory for testing. Normally submitting to a blood draw is voluntary but in some instances the driver may not be given an option (i.e. if the driver is unconscious).

There are now many States that authorize search warrants to obtain blood samples. Typically this occurs if the driver refuses the blood draw and the law enforcement officer requests a search warrant from a Judge. However, it is the practice of some law enforcement to circumvent the request for blood and proceed directly to the application for a search warrant. Once the Judge authorizes the search warrant the officer may demand the blood be drawn lawfully from the driver and used as evidence.

There has been much contention regarding whether blood may be drawn from a driver without the driver's consent and without a search warrant. In 2013 came some degree of clarity on this issue, although the language delivered still seems to provide many areas of confusion and disagreement. In *Missouri v. McNeely* the Supreme Court of the United States ruled that police officers must "usually" obtain a warrant before conducting blood draws on suspected impaired drivers. (1) The Court stated the following:

> If there is time to secure a warrant before blood can be drawn, the police must seek one. If an officer could reasonably conclude that there is not sufficient time to seek and receive a warrant, or he applies for one but does not receive a response before blood can be drawn, a warrantless blood draw may ensue. (2)

The language the Court used in *Missouri v. McNeely* clearly can be potentially abused by law enforcement so the issue over warrantless blood draws does not seem to have been solved by this seminal case. Further, this case dealt with alcohol and the natural metabolism of the drug and the importance of obtaining evidence before the elimination of alcohol from the body. It will be interesting to see over the upcoming years if States attempt to circumvent this Supreme Court ruling by interpreting this case as an alcohol only case and therefore not applying to marijuana or other drugs. When broadly read this case seems to apply to any driving under the influence case involving any drug, including alcohol and marijuana, as all drugs have a natural metabolism, albeit at different rates.

The Blood Draw

Many states demand that only a licensed physician, or an individual operating under the delegation of a licensed physician, who is qualified to withdraw blood and is acting in a medical environment, may withdraw blood at a peace officer's request to determine the amount of alcohol or drugs in a person's blood. The phrase "qualified to draw blood" is rather broadly defined however, and a person can be qualified to draw blood by having some level of education, training, or experience.

Similar to breath testing, there are administrative rules that cover blood testing. Such rules require how the test results should be expressed, the acceptable techniques for blood testing, the calibration of the test equipment, and the collection and handling of the blood samples.

Additionally, case law has evolved to define what the requesting party must prove when attempting to validate a blood sample as evidence. These requirements may vary from State to State but can be generally summarized as needing proof (1.) that the blood was timely taken, (2.) from a particular identified body, (3.) by an authorized licensed physician, medical technologist, or registered nurse designated by a licensed physician, (4.) that the instruments used were sterile, (5.) that the blood taken was properly preserved or kept, (6.) and labeled, and (7.) if transported or sent, the method and procedures used therein, (8.) the method and procedures used in conducting the test, and (9.) that the identity of the person or persons under whose supervision the tests were conducted is established.

Handling the Blood

States that utilize the blood draw as a means of gathering evidence of possible alcohol or drug intoxication have available to them blood analysis kits. These kits are commercially packaged and available for blood testing.

Proper protocol must be used to collect the blood sample, otherwise the blood analysis will be flawed and have no evidentiary value. The American Medical

Association suggests the following procedures:

1. Hypodermic needles and syringes (must) be sterile and disposable. When reusable equipment is utilized, it should neither be cleaned with nor stored in alcohol or other volatile solvents.
2. Only a chemically cleaned, dry tube or vial with inert stopper should be used. Neither alcohol nor volatile solvents should be used to clean them. The tubes and vials should contain an anticoagulant (recommended are fluoride, citrate, oxalate and heparin), and a preservative (recommended are fluoride and mercury salt.) (3)

The anticoagulant in the vial is designed to prevent the sample from clotting inside the vial. The preservative prevents yeast growth, which may cause the blood to ferment, thereby increasing the concentration of ethyl alcohol in the sample. Finally, the sample should be refrigerated during storage with 1% sodium fluoride. Lesser concentrations may allow microorganisms to grow, thereby inhibiting glycolysis. (4)

Areas of concern or inquiry as to the validity of the blood sample include:

- The collection of the blood sample by the nurse, doctor or phlebotomist;
- Use of an appropriate blood collection kit;

- The transportation of the blood;
- The storage of the blood;
- The preparation of the blood for testing;
- The testing of the blood;
- The chain of command in handling the blood;
- The reporting of the blood alcohol level.

Blood Specimen Collection – the Legal Checklist

The phlebotomist drawing the blood from a suspect should follow the steps noted below in order to ensure the specimen will be accurately analyzed and the chain of custody will be intact. Any significant deviation from these steps may raise questions about the accuracy of the sample analysis.

Step One: Remove all components from the blood alcohol kit box.

Step Two: Assemble needle to holder.

Step Three: Apply tourniquet and prepare venipuncture site using only a non-alcoholic antiseptic. *Note:* Some antiseptics contain alcohol as a solvent.

Step Four: Following normal hospital/clinic procedure, withdraw blood specimen from subject. The arm should be in a downward or lowered position, while the tube should be in a slanted position with the stopper in the highest position.

Step Five: As the tube begins to fill, the tourniquet should be removed. The contents of the tube should not contact the stopper. Special attention should be given to the arm position in order to prevent possible backflow from the tube and the possibility of adverse reaction to the subject.

Step Six: When the tube fill is complete, blood should cease to flow. The tube should be removed from the holder and any additional tubes should be placed into the holder following the same procedure.

Step Seven: When sampling is completed, the needle/holder assembly should be removed in its entirety. A dry, sterile compress should be applied to the venipuncture site. The arm should be elevated.

Step Eight: To assure proper mixing of the chemicals in the tube with the blood, each tube should be slowly and completely inverted at least five times immediately after blood collection. *The tube should not be shaken vigorously.*

Step Nine: The subject's name or other identifying information should be placed on the tube.

Step Ten: Any paperwork associated with the blood kit must be filled out and signed by the person withdrawing the blood.

Step Eleven: The blood tubes should be properly packaged and placed in the blood kit. A liquid-absorbing packet should be included with the test tubes to determine if any leakage occurs during transportation.

Step Twelve: A biohazard label should be affixed to the exterior of the blood kit. The kit is now ready for transportation to the laboratory for analysis.

Note: Normally, a complete toxicology screen requires two tubes of blood (20 ml)

The Testing Procedure

Most every component of the DUI process involves procedures that law enforcement (and toxicology labs) must adhere to. Blood testing in the DUI realm is no different and every state has procedures and practices outlined statutorily and by their State toxicology office. To maintain the integrity of the test results and be admissible in court requires the prosecutor to prove the administrative procedures were properly followed.

The testing procedure for blood employs a process called has chromatography. Gas chromatography is defined as "a process in which a chemical mixture carried by a liquid or gas is separated into components as a result of differential distribution of the solutes as they flow around or over a stationary liquid or solid phase." (5) In a court room environment the testimony of an expert would prove invaluable in explaining gas chromatography and its application to the blood testing process. Such experts are necessary for the prosecution and defense counsel alike.

CHAPTER 6

Marijuana Dependency and Treatment

Each year, approximately 20,000 to 30,000 new marijuana users in the United States develop drug dependency within the first two years of use. It may surprise many to learn that of all illicit drugs, marijuana had the highest rate of past year dependence or abuse in the year 2008, followed by pain relievers and cocaine. (1) Peak initiation for cannabis use is at age 18, and ten years later, 8% of users are marijuana-dependent. (2)

Drug dependence has a biological component in which the body's equilibrium is disturbed after repeated or chronic exposure to a particular drug to such a degree that physical symptoms develop after abrupt withdrawal of the drug. Withdrawal symptoms from marijuana may include chills, muscle pain, decreased appetite and food intake, disturbed sleep, and craving. The psychological component of drug dependence, defined as an intense craving or desire to repeatedly use a drug or obtain a drug because it produces a feeling of improved well-being, is a component of addictive behavior. Addiction to marijuana, like that for other substances of abuse, has genetic, psychosocial, and environmental influences, and is characterized by impaired control over drug use or compulsive drug use, continued drug use despite harm to self and others, and cravings. An addict may not fully comprehend the totality of harm caused by their drug-using and drug-seeking behaviors, and they may not agree that they need to stop using.

Treatment for marijuana addiction was largely ignored until the 1990s primarily because dependency with prolonged use had not been well documented. It is now known that abrupt cessation of marijuana use results in withdrawal symptoms that disappear if drug use is resumed – the class definition of drug dependency. Furthermore, this phenomenon occurs in all animal species tested in the laboratory setting. (3) Nevertheless, the need for marijuana addiction treatment is not uniformly recognized throughout the health care profession, and treatment is considered unnecessary or is given a slight nod with mild recommendations: "for patients experiencing significant discomfort, treatment is supportive." (4)

Data from drug addiction treatment programs provide proof that marijuana addiction does exist. According to the *Treatment Episode Data Set*, a national database of admissions data from detoxification and rehabilitation facilities that treat alcohol and drug abuse, from the *Substance Abuse and Mental Health Service Administration*, for the year 2007, marijuana dependence was the third most common reason for admission to a drug treatment program (behind alcohol and opiate dependence). Data analysis also indicates that marijuana dependence increased during the 10-year period from 1997-2007. Findings from the 2008 *National Survey on Drug Use and Health* revealed that an estimated 947,000 persons aged 12 and older reported receiving treatment for marijuana use in 2008. (5)

Treatment Approaches

Psychotherapy and pharmacotherapy are the two treatment options for marijuana dependence, although at this time, pharmacologic approaches are experimental. (6) The most common psychotherapeutic, or behavioral, intervention approaches for the management of marijuana dependence are similar to those shown to be effective in treating alcohol dependence. (7) These approaches include cognitive behavioral therapy, motivational enhancement, and motivational incentives, and can be provided on an outpatient basis, meaning that hospitalization or treatment facility admission is not required (8). Compared with cocaine and other drugs of abuse known to have high risk of dependency, marijuana consistently scores lower on scales that measure effects and impairment. (11) Like other drugs of abuse, total abstinence from marijuana use after treatment is difficult to achieve and relapse rates are high. For this reason, pharmacologic intervention with medications is warranted and several targets have been identified and used to some success. However, to date managing marijuana dependence with medications has not been a highly successful form of treatment. There has been some research to suggest that a combination of a cannabinoid agonist medication with lofexidine (a medication approved in the United Kingdom for the treatment of opioid withdrawal) produced results in improving sleep patterns and decreased marijuana withdrawal, craving, and relapse in daily marijuana smokers relative to either medication alone. Additionally, there have also been relatively recent findings about the fundamentals of the endogenous cannabinoid system to suggest that medication may one day be available to block THC's intoxicating effects. Such medication may prevent relapse by reducing or eliminating the appeal of marijuana use, although this remains very speculative at the present time. For now, medication to suppress marijuana dependence is a definitely a work in progress.

Bibliography

Chapter 1

1. Kalant, H. *Adverse Effects of Cannabis on Health: An Update of the Literature since 1996.* Progress in Neuro-Psychopharmacology and Biological Psychiatry 28, 5 (August 2004).
2. Grotenhermen, F. *The Toxicology of Cannabis and Cannabis Prohibition.* Chemistry and Biodiversity. (August 2007).
3. Wilson, N and Cadet, J.L. *Comorbid Mood, Psychosis, and Marijuana Abuse Disorders: A theoretical Review.* Journal of Addiction Diseases. (October 2009).
4. *United States v. Oakland Cannabis Buyers' Coop* 532 U.S. 483 (2001).

5. *Gonzales v. Raich.* 545 U.S. 1 (2005).
6. Joy, J.E., Watson, S.J. Jr., Bensons, J.A. Jr. *Marijuana and Medicine: Assessing the Science Base.* Washington D.C.: National Academy Press. (1999)

Chapter 2

1. Albery IP, Strang J, Gossop M, Griffiths P. *Illicit drugs and driving: prevalence, beliefs and accident involvement among a cohort of current out-of-treatment drug users.* Drug Alcohol Depend. 2000 Feb 1;58(1–2):197–204.
2. Macdonald S, DeSouza A, Mann R, Chipman M. *Driving behavior of alcohol, cannabis, and cocaine abuse treatment clients and population controls.* Am J Drug Alcohol Abuse. 2004 May;30(2):429–444.
3. McLean S, Parsons RS, Chesterman RB, Dineen R, Johnson MG, Davies NW. *Drugs, alcohol and road accidents in Tasmania.* Med J Aust. 1987 Jul 6;147(1):6–11.
4. Soderstrom CA, Dischinger PC, Kerns TJ, Trifillis AL. *Marijuana and other drug use among automobile and motorcycle drivers treated at a trauma center.* Accid Anal Prev. 1995 Feb;27(1):131–135.
5. Moskowitz H. *Marihuana and driving.* Accid Anal Prev. 1985 Aug;17(4):323–345.

6. Hall W. *The health and psychological consequences of cannabis use.* Canberra: Australian Government Publication Service; 1994.
7. Kurzthaler I, Hummer M, Miller C, et al. *Effect of cannabis use on cognitive functions and driving ability.* J Clin Psychiatry. 1999 Jun;60(6):395–399.
8. Liguori A, Gatto CP, Robinson JH. *Effects of marijuana on equilibrium, psychomotor performance, and simulated driving.* Behav Pharmacol. 1998 Nov;9(7):599–609.
9. Berghaus G, Guo B. *Medicines and driver fitness--findings from a meta-analysis of experimental studies as basic information to patients, physicians and experts.* In: Kloeden C, McLean A, editors. Alcohol, Drugs, and Traffic Safety--T95: *Proceedings of the 13th International Conference on Alcohol, Drugs and Traffics Safety;* 1995; Adelaide, Australia. 1995. pp. 295–300.
10. Foltin R, Evans S. *Performance Effects of Drugs of Abuse: A Methodological Survey.* Human Psychopharmacology. 1993;8:9–19.
11. Chesher G. *The Effects of Alcohol and Marijuana in Combination: A Review.* Alcohol, Drugs and Driving. 1986;2:105–119
12. Australian Institute of Health and Welfare. *2007 National Drug Strategy Household Survey: Detailed findings.* AIHW cat. no. PHE 107. Canberra: AIHW (Drug Statistics Series No. 22). (2008)

13. Walsh, J.M. & Mann, R.E. On the high road: *Driving under the influence of cannabis in Ontario*. Canadian Journal of Public Health *90*, 260-263. (1999)

14. Adlaf, E.M., Mann, R.E. & Paglia, A. *Drinking, cannabis use and driving among Ontario students*. Canadian Medical Association Journal *168*, 565-566. (2003)

15. Simpson, H., Singhal, D., Vanlaar, W., & Mayhew, D. *The road safety monitor: Drugs and driving*. Ontario: Traffic Injury Research Foundation. (2006)

16. EMCDDA. *Drug use, impaired driving and traffic accidents. EMCDDA Insights Series No 8*. Luxembourg: Office for Official Publications of the European Communities. (2008b)

17. Neale, J., McKeganey, N., Hay, G., & Oliver, J. *Recreational drug use and driving: A qualitative study*: Scottish Executive Central Research Unit. (2000).

18. Asbridge, M., Poulin, C. & Donato, A. *Motor vehicle collision risk and driving under the influence of cannabis: Evidence from adolescents in Atlantic Canada*. Accident Analysis & Prevention 37, 1025-1034. (2005)

19. Terry, P. & Wright, K. *Self-reported driving behaviour and attitudes towards driving under the influence of cannabis among three different user*

groups in England. Addictive Behaviors 30, 619-626. (2005)

20. Kelly, E., Darke, S. & Ross, J. *A review of drug use and driving: Epidemiology, impairment, risk factor and risk perceptions.* Drug and Alcohol Review *23*, 319-344. (2004)

21. Turner, B.M.A. *Sex, drugs, and driving: The effects of marijuana.* Turner, Beth Marie Anderson: U Iowa, US. (2007)

22. Ashton, C.H. *Adverse effects of cannabis and cannabinoids.* British Journal of Anaesthesia *83*, 637-649. (1999)

23. Ramaekers, J.G., Moeller, M., van Ruitenbeek, P., Theunissen, E., Schneider, E., & Kauert, G. *Cognition and motor control as a function of Delta -sup-9-THC concentration in serum and oral fluid: Limits of impairment.* Drug and Alcohol Dependence 85, 114-122. (2006)

24. Ramaekers, J.G., Kauert, G., van Ruitenbeek, P., Theunissen, E., Schneider, E., & Moeller, M. *High-potency marijuana impairs executive function and inhibitory motor control.* Neuropsychopharmacology 31, 2296-2303. (2006)

25. EMCDDA. *A cannabis reader: Global issues and local experiences*, Monograph series 8, Volume 2. Lisbon: European Monitoring Centre for Drugs and Addiction. (2008a).

26. Smiley, A. *Marijuana: On-Road and Driving-Simulator Studies.* (1986)
27. Ronen, A., Gershon, P., Drobiner, H., Rabinovich, A., Bar-Hamburger, R., Mechoulam, R., et al. *Effects of THC on driving performance, physiological state and subjective feelings relative to alcohol.* Accident Analysis & Prevention 40, 926-934. (2008)
28. Papafotiou, K., Stough, C. & Nathan, P. *Detection of cannabis-induced impairments with sobriety testing.* Hawthorn: Swinburne University. (2002)
29. Robbe, HWJ. *Marijuana and Actual Driving Performance*, HWJ Robbe Institute for Human Psychopharmacology (1993)
30. Drummer, O.H., Gerostamoulos, J., Batziris, H., Chu, M., Caplehorn, J.R., Robertson, M.D., et al. *The involvement of drugs in drivers of motor vehicles killed in Australian road traffic crashes.* Accident Analysis & Prevention 36, 239-248. (2004)
31. Laumon, B., Gadegbeku, B., Martin, J.-L., Biecheler, M.-B., & the SAM Group. *Cannabis intoxication and fatal road crashes in France: Population based case-control study.* BMJ 331, 1371-1373. (2005)
32. Crancer A, Jr, Dille JM, Delay JC, Wallace JE, Haykin MD. *Comparison of the effects of marihuana and alcohol on simulated driving performance.* Science. 1969 May 16;164(881):851–854.

33. Dott A. *Effect of marijuana on risk acceptance in a simulated passing task*. Washington, DC: US Government Printing Office; 1971.
34. Rafaelsen L, Christrup H, Bech P, Rafaelsen OJ. *Effects of cannabis and alcohol on psychological tests*. Nature. 1973 Mar 9;242(5393):117–118.
35. Smiley A, Moskowitz H, Ziedman K. *Driving simulator studies of marijuana alone and in combination with alcohol*. Paper presented at: 25th Conference of the American Association for Automotive Medicine; 1981.
36. Moskowitz H, Hulbert S, McGlothlin W. *Marijuana: Effects on simulated driving performance*. Accid Anal Prev. 1976;8:45–50.
37. Casswell S. *Cannabis and alcohol: Effects on closed-course driving behavior*. Paper presented at: Seventh International Conference on Alcohol, Drugs, and Traffic Safety; 1977; Melbourne, Australia.

Chapter 3

1. NHTSA, U.S. Department of Transportation. *DWI Detection and Standardized Field Sobriety Testing, Student Manual*. HS 178 R8/06, Page VII-7-8 (2006)
2. *The Effect of Alcohol on Human Performance: A Classification and Integration of Research Findings*.

American Institutes for Research. Page iv. (May 1973)

3. Adams, Raymond D. & Victor, Maurice. *Disorders of Ocular Movement and Pupillary Function.* Principles of Neurology. Ch.13, 117 (4th ed. 1991)

4. Forkiotis, C.J. *Optometric Exercise: The Scientific Basis for Alcohol Gaze Nystagmus.* 59 Curriculum II, No. 7 at 9 (April 1987);

5. Good, Gregory W. & Augsburger, Arol R. *Use of Horizontal Gaze Nystagmus as a Part of Roadside Sobriety Testing.* 63 Am. J. of Optometry & Physiological Optics 467, 469 (1986);

6. Stapleton, June M. et al. *Effects of Alcohol and Other Psychotropic Drugs on Eye Movements: Relevance to Traffic Safety.* 47 Q.J. Stud. on Alcohol 426, 430 (1986)

7. Pangman. *Horizontal Gaze Nystagmus: Voodoo Science.* 2 DWI J. 1, 3-4 (1987)

8. Cole, S., Nowaczyk, R. *Field Sobriety Tests: Are they Designed for Failure?* Percept Mot. Skills. Page 79 (1994)

9. Stuster, Jack and Burn, Marcelline. *Validation of the Standardized Field Sobriety Test Battery at BACs Below .10 Percent.* DOT-HS-808-839 6. Page 28 (1998)

10. Snapper, K.J., Seaver, D.A.., Schwartz, J.P. *An Assessment of Behavioral Tests to Detect Impaired*

Drivers. Final Report, DOTHS-806-211. Pages 2-7 (1981)
11. Department of California Highway Patrol. *Driving Under the Influence Enforcement Manual*. Pages 2-12 (1995)
12. Cole, S., Kulis, I., Nawaczyk, R., *NHTSA and FSTs: True Lies and False Advertising*. DWI Journal, Law & Science. 12:3. Pages 1-8. (March 1977).
13. Booker JL. *End-position nystagmus as an indicator of ethanol intoxication*. Sci Justice. 41(2):113-116. Page 113 (April-June 2001)
14. ImObersteg, A. *The Romberg Balance Test: Differentiating Normal Sway from Alcohol-Induced Sway*. DWI Journal, Law & Science, Vol. 18, No. 5 (May, 2003)
15. Anderson, Theodore E. et al. *Field Evaluation of a Behavioral Test Battery for DWI*. DOT-HS-806-475 (1983)
16. Sworn Testimony of Marcelline Burns in *State v. Meador*, 674 So. 2d 826, 834 (Fla. Dist. Ct. App. 1996)
17. K. Papafotiou . J. D. Carter . C. Stough. *An evaluation of the sensitivity of the Standardised Field Sobriety Tests (SFSTs) to detect impairment due to marijuana intoxication.* Psychopharmacology (2005)

Chapter 4

1. Jolly, David N. *DUI/DWI: The History of Driving Under the Influence*. Outskirts Press (2009)
2. American Prosecutors Research Institute. *The Drug Evaluation and Classification (DEC) Program. Targeting Hardcore Impaired Drivers*. Page 2 (October 2004)
3. American Prosecutors Research Institute. *The Drug Evaluation and Classification (DEC) Program. Targeting Hardcore Impaired Drivers*. Page 2 (October 2004)

Chapter 5

1. *Missouri v. McNeely,* 133 S.Ct. 832 (2013)
2. *Id.*
3. American Medical Association, Alcohol and the Impaired Driver: *A Manual of the Medical-Legal Aspects of Chemical Tests for Intoxication with Supplement on Breath/Alcohol Tests* (1976 reprint).
4. Kaye. *"The Collection and Handling of Blood Alcohol Specimen,"* 75 American Journal of Clinical Pathology 743 (1980).
5. Merriam-Webster Dictionary.

Chapter 6

1. National Admissions to Substance Abuse Treatment Services, DASIS Services: S-47. *Substance Abuse and Mental Health Services Administration.* Treatment Episode Data Set (TEDS): 1997-2007. . http://www.oas.samhsa.gov/copies.cfm (2010).
2. Wagner, F.A.., Anthony, J.C. *From first drug use to drug dependence; developmental periods of risk for dependence upon marijuana, cocaine, and alcohol.* Neuropsychopharmacology. (April 2002)
3. Beers, M.H. et al. *The Merck Manual of Diagnosis and Therapy.* 18th ed. Merck Research Laboratories (2006).
4. Merck Sharp & Dohme Corp.. *Marijuana (Cannabis): Drug Use and Dependence.* Merck Manual, Professional Edition.
5. *SAMHSA, Results from the 2008 National Survey on Drug Use and Health* (2009).
6. Elkashef, et al. *Marijuana Neurobiology and Treatment.* Substance Abuse 29, 3 (2008).
7. National Institute on Drug Abuse. *Medications Development for the Treatment of Cannabis – Related Disorders (R01).* http://grants.nih.gov/grants/guide/pa-files/PA-070365.html (2010)
8. Hathaway, A.D. et al. *Cannabis Dependence as a Primary Drug Use- Related Problem: The Case*

for Harm Reduction-Oriented Treatment Options. Substance Use and Misuse 44, 7. (2009)

9. Gouzoulis-Mayfrank, E. *Dual diagnosis psychosis and substance use disorders: Theoretical foundations and treatment. Z Kinder Jugendpsychiatr Psychother* 36(4):245–253 (2008)